Live to Air

Live to Air

The Craig Broadcast Story

Chris Wood

Douglas & McIntyre
Vancouver/Toronto

For Richard Green and Brian Toller,
who introduced me to the Trent University Radio Service
and permanently set back my academic career

00 01 02 03 04 5 4 3 2 1

Douglas & McIntyre Ltd.
2323 Quebec Street, Suite 201
Vancouver, British Columbia V5T 4S7

Canadian Cataloguing in Publication Data
Wood, Chris, 1953–
Live to Air

Includes index.
ISBN 1-55054-774-7
1. Craig Broadcast Systems—History. I. Title.
HE8689.9.C3W66 2000 384.54′06′571 C99-911328-3

Cover and text design by Aitken+Blakeley
Front cover photograph by Keith Levit; back cover photograph courtesy of the Craig family
Typeset by Brenda and Neil West, BN Typographics West
Printed and bound in Canada by Friesens
Printed on acid-free paper ∞

We gratefully acknowledge the financial support of the Canada Council for the Arts, the British Columbia Ministry of Tourism, Small Business and Culture, and the Government of Canada through the Book Publishing Industry Development Program (BPDIP) for our publishing activities.

Contents

Prologue

Southwestern Manitoba is far lovelier than I remember. It's high summer as I drive toward Riding Mountain National Park, three hours to the west and north of Winnipeg. The land is wide, but it has enough of a roll and rise to keep the eye interested. The visible richness of the soil surprises me. It is the colour of dark chocolate where a ploughed field stands out against soft splashes of green—lighter tones where wheat tosses in the breeze, darker at the treeline and the windbreaks around many of the homes.

Overhead, low cloud hides the sun. Now and again, wind sets tiny whitecaps reaching across the blue-black surface of sloughs. As the clouds open for a moment, shafts of sunlight blaze down onto fields of suddenly flaming canola. Away to the south, rain showers show up against the dark horizon like grey brush-strokes. The clouds there flicker dully with interior lightning.

I try to imagine this countryside in winter. In the 1920s. With bad roads and people still in buggies. No phones. No light after sundown apart from coal-oil lamps. The silence broken only by the wind. The hunger for word of the larger world. No wonder folks embraced radio so eagerly.

Miles ahead, a single red light blinks against the plum-coloured sky. A broadcasting tower. In this setting, there is something otherworldly about it. I think of the electricity in the air, and the mystery (to me) of how a 300-metre, ruby-tipped wand squirts out invisible, weightless wriggles that somehow reassemble themselves into Shania Twain's voice filling my rent-a-car. If I were home and watching TV, those wriggles would even show me her belly button. If we were not so jaded, we would marvel daily at the miracle of it all.

The pioneers of "wireless" didn't wear pointed hats covered with stars, but they might have. They did sell their share of snake oil. But then, broadcasting has always been a funny business, built mostly on faith: in the invisible laws of physics, an invisible audience, the persuasive power of advertising. There is a special audacity about beginning a broadcasting endeavour from scratch, about rolling the dice on that moment when the magic machinery stirs and sends out the first sound, the first picture, expanding outward like ripples on water.

John B. Craig of Brandon, Manitoba, possessed that kind of audacity, and he instilled it in the generations of Craigs that followed. Like their grandfather, the three Craig men who run the family business today love broadcasting with a passion that transcends the bottom line. As Boyd Craig told me unequivocally over beer in a bar: "I'm not a money guy. I'm a broadcaster."

Cue the lightning.

1

Sign-on

Randall Moffat welcomed his guest warmly and invited the older man to take a seat. For several minutes the two executives relaxed in Moffat's expensively panelled and carpeted office, chatting about the industry in which both had come of age. Moffat was well acquainted with his visitor, Stuart Craig. Craig's father, John Craig, had gone into broadcasting in the same era as Moffat's own father, Lloyd, during the buoyantly optimistic years that came just after the Second World War.

Since then, Moffat Communications Ltd., of which Randall was now president, had evolved into a mid-sized public company headquartered in Winnipeg. Its principal asset was that city's CKY Television, an affiliate of the national CTV network. Although the Craigs had followed a different course, keeping their business private, their principal holding was also a television station: CKX-TV in Brandon, Manitoba, a CBC affiliate. Relations between the two families had always been cordial. For more than a decade, in fact, the two had been partners in bringing CTV programs from Moffat's Winnipeg station to Brandon, where they were broadcast from the same antenna tower as the Craig station's CBC shows.

Now that friendly dynamic was about to change. Five months earlier, on May 8, 1986, the agency that awards broadcasting licences in Canada, the Canadian Radio-television and Telecommunications Commission—better known as the CRTC—had given Craig's company, Western Manitoba Broadcasters Ltd., permission to launch Manitoba's first new television station in more than a dozen years. CHMI-TV would technically be based in Portage la Prairie, a farming and service town 75 kilometres west of Moffat's central Winnipeg office. His new station, Craig had assured the CRTC, would neither solicit nor accept advertising from local Winnipeg retailers.

But despite that collegial gesture, there was little doubt in either executive's mind about the real nature of the game that was about to begin. Hitherto, Winnipeggers had been able to choose among three local television services: Moffat's CKY, a local CBC outlet and CKND-TV, an independent station controlled by former politician Israel (Izzy) Asper. Among them, the stations shared a market that each year spun off television advertising worth close to $50 million.

Now Stuart Craig was crashing the party. The second-generation broadcaster from Brandon was about to launch a stealth assault on Manitoba's richest broadcast prize. Winnipeg's existing broadcasters could look forward to their audiences—and their revenues—shrinking in direct proportion to the Craig venture's success.

Randy Moffat had been keeping close tabs on his friend's progress. As the conversation turned to business, he let loose a carefully aimed barb. "So," Moffat asked Stu Craig, "what are you going to do for a tower and transmitter?" As the younger man knew full well, the two essential pieces of hardware upon which all of Stuart Craig's hopes depended—CHMI-TV's antenna tower and its massive, Ontario-built Larcan signal transmitter—were still lying in sections and crates across the new station's freshly poured concrete floor. Sign-on was set for October 17, 1986, just ten days away.

"Don't worry about our transmitter," Craig tossed back. "We'll be there."

For Stuart Craig, the road thus far had been long and sometimes frustrating. Western Manitoba Broadcasters Ltd. had eyed the Winnipeg market with envy for decades. Although Brandon—a town that sits on the Trans-Canada Highway two-thirds of the way from Winnipeg to the Saskatchewan border—was Manitoba's second-largest city, its 30,000 souls were a tiny fraction of the provincial capital's 650,000 people. Twice before, Craig's company had applied to the CRTC for broadcast licences that would give WestMan access to the larger market. On one occasion, the CRTC awarded the valuable permit instead to Asper's CanWest Television Inc. On another, the commission simply turned down all the applications before it. Finally, in May of 1986, the regulator had approved WestMan's third bid, awarding the company a licence to broadcast on VHF Channel 13—the last unassigned off-air VHF television channel in that area of Manitoba. The licence did not give WestMan the go-ahead to put the new station in Winnipeg proper. But as both Craig and the CRTC knew, the signal from WestMan's proposed Portage la Prairie studios would beam powerfully across the intervening flatland directly into the larger centre.

As if to make up for lost years, Stu Craig set a blistering pace for getting the new television station up and running. WestMan planned to put its signal on the air within 162 days of getting the licence—half the time most broadcasters would allow for such a project. So tight was the schedule, in fact, that Moffat was not the only one questioning whether the Brandon group could pull it off. Quite a few potential advertisers had refused to buy time on the new station's initial schedule because they didn't believe it had a hope in hell of making its launch date.

But the naysayers had underestimated Craig's Scots determination. The CRTC issued its decision on a Thursday. By the following Monday, Stuart and WestMan chief engineer Lawrence Dubois were examining sites for a studio building and transmission tower at Portage la Prairie. Soon Stuart and Drew Craig—at twenty-eight, the eldest of the three Craig sons, who were all increasingly involved in the family business—were on their way to Toronto. Their mission: Find something to fill the air time WestMan had just won *and* a transmitter to get these shows on the air.

"It was all done in one day," Stuart would recall later in amazement. "There were some very funny meetings. We'd ask [the program distributors] what was available for Manitoba, and they'd say 'This and this,' and we'd say 'Okay.' By the time we went to bed that night, we had a whole lot of programs bought and we had a transmitter."

Other purchases followed in dizzying succession: cameras, videotape machines, special-effects generators, control-room consoles—all in all, well over a million dollars' worth of studio and broadcast equipment. Manitoba Hydro was contracted to build a three-kilometre power line to deliver electricity to the transmitter site. Stuart, Drew and Miles Craig (the youngest son, then twenty-five) spent hours interviewing applicants for dozens of positions that needed to be filled—everything from news anchor to station janitor. (Middle brother Boyd, twenty-six, was back in Brandon, holding the fort at the family's existing television and radio stations.) Still, it was not until August 11 that Portage la Prairie officials finally approved a building permit for the station's proposed studios. Actual construction of an all-steel building didn't start until September 5. Sign-on was just six weeks away.

By Thanksgiving weekend, the building was up. Randy Moffat's doubts notwithstanding, so too were a tower and a transmission antenna. It would be three months more before administration and sales offices were finished, furnished and decorated. But Drew Craig, already an experienced TV producer, was pushing a dozen newly hired reporters and on-air hosts to complete a sixty-minute special broadcast to launch the new service. In Winnipeg, hundreds of thousands of dollars' worth of advertising splashed the new station's identity—MTN, for Manitoba Television Network—across everything from bus shelters and billboards to the morning paper and local radio: anything the Craigs could think of to let every living soul in the Manitoba capital city know that something new and exciting was coming to their television screens on October 17.

At last the day arrived. Engineer Dubois, the Craigs and most of the senior staff were nearing exhaustion from the forced-march pace of preparations. But all indicators were finally green for the station's launch that evening.

Then a telephone rang, and someone called Dubois to pick up. His smile faded quickly. On the line was an engineer, calling from the site of the new transmitter. Somehow, high-voltage electricity had strayed beyond its prescribed pathway in the complex guts of the transmitter equipment, unleashing a mini–lightning storm of electric-blue arcs across a critical internal cavity. MTN's spanking new transmitter was stone cold dead.

Dubois and Stuart Craig raced to the tower site. By the time they got there, the transmitter was in pieces on the floor. A deeply apologetic Larcan technician offered an explanation: it looked as though someone at the company's Toronto factory had used a single iron screw in place of the correct brass one when assembling the unit. The effect was to draw a tongue of high-voltage juice across an internal space occupied by several large vacuum tubes, leaving the Teflon-coated surface scorched black with soot. The technician assured Craig that the company was rushing a new part to the site. It was scheduled to be on a flight due at the Winnipeg airport—an hour's drive away—by six o'clock.

Six o'clock! With all of Winnipeg watching for the new station to light up at 7:00, that wasn't going to be good enough. But experience does count for something. The Craig family may have been new to Winnipeg, but they were hardly neophytes in the broadcasting game. Neither was engineer Dubois. Between them, Dubois and Stuart Craig possessed more than fifty years of broadcast expertise. And as it happened, they had seen precisely this phenomenon before, even if the man from Larcan had not.

Some years earlier, a similar transmitter, used to rebroadcast CKX-TV's signal from a southern Manitoba high point named Baldy Mountain, had suffered an identical fault, knocking the station off the air for several days. The problem had been annoying at the time, but now it was to pay a huge dividend. Craig and Dubois believed they knew how to return the transmitter to service long before the spare part arrived. The fix would require several hours of labour and some unusual supplies, but it could be done.

"We went down to the hardware store," recalled Stu Craig, "and bought some Bon Ami and some Windex and some clean cloths, and began to get the thing cleaned up." Once the cavity's internal surface was again polished to a mirror-like sheen, technicians reassembled the transmitter and cautiously switched it on. With a series of clicks and the thrum of rising high-voltage current, the machine awakened.

They did not dare run the unit up to full power. But even tuned to about one-third of its strength, it seemed capable of putting out a steady signal without arcing. It would be enough, barely, to allow MTN to keep its heavily advertised date with Winnipeg. (As things turned out, the part from Larcan did not arrive until several weeks later.)

Back at the station, there had been problems for Drew and his team too. The launch special, a colourful, pretaped mix of segments extolling MTN and including the station's first local news package, was scheduled to run for an hour. But there were complications: missed cues among the production team, whose members had yet to settle into any kind of routine, and all-thumbs performances from technicians who were bone-weary and unfamiliar with their shiny new equipment. As the 7:00 p.m. sign-on loomed, it became increasingly apparent they would not get a clean mix of the program on tape by the time it was due on air. "At a quarter after six," Drew concedes, "I got a little worried."

In desperation, he decided to gamble. MTN's very first show would have to be mixed live-to-air. If they fell flat on their faces, they would do so with all of southern Manitoba watching. As the seconds ticked down to 7:00, a control-room operator raised one more small point. "What time is it?" he wanted to know.

Drew Craig looked up in shock. In their rush, they had forgotten to hook up the control-room clock. "Okay," Drew decided aloud, "we'll use my watch."

Several blocks away, in the Manitobah [sic] Inn, Stuart Craig was shaking the hand of Portage la Prairie's mayor, confidently welcoming him to a splashy reception to celebrate the new station's launch. As seven o'clock arrived, all eyes turned to the television sets placed strategically around the room. The second hand on a score of wristwatches swept past the top of the hour. On cue, the screens came to life.

Back at the studio, Drew Craig's tension finally eased sixty minutes later. "We assembled that first show right on the money—to the tenth of a second," he would always remember. "The folks back at the party had no idea."

For Canada, more than for most countries, geography is destiny. This land of astonishing physical variety, in all its dangerous beauty, its rugged intractability, its sheer bloody *size,* has shaped the lives of the people who inhabit it. The first humans to occupy this part of the planet felt such profound oneness with root and branch, stone and water, that many aboriginal societies possessed no more specific name for themselves than "The People Who Live Here." The first non-aboriginals to venture across the Atlantic thought it well worth the terror for the plunder from this "new-found" land: fish, fur, timber. Later migrants came to put down roots, agog that so much space appeared to be empty and unclaimed—a view encouraged by the federal government at the expense of the First Nations. Later still, a Canadian prime minister would visit China and joke that while some scholars say that ancient nation is afflicted with too much history, Canada has the opposite problem: too much geography.

But if so much wide-open space can be a curse, it has also spurred some Canadians to acts of heroism and genius—and a few to extraordinary wealth. The extent to which Canada broke trail for the rest of the world in the conquest of distance is too often forgotten. That Yank, Thomas Alva Edison, may have given the world electric light and captured music on wax cylinders, but Canadians gave it radio and the telephone (and, some insist, the television as well).

The formative national enterprise of our first half-century was a railroad. The corresponding achievement of our second, some argue, was a public broadcasting system. In 1962, the communications satellite *Alouette* made Canada the third country in the world (after the two superpowers of the era, the United States and the former Soviet Union) to establish a presence in space. This national preoccupation is reflected daily in our politics. After matters of finance and the perennial debate over Quebec, no single subject provokes more heated argument in this huge land than the topic of moving stuff across it—whether people, goods or information. In the nineteenth century, it was subsidies to the railway that divided public opinion. At the dawn of the twenty-first, it is whether to let two national airlines merge into one.

The longest-running irritant in our relationship with the United States is all about communicating as well. Canadians have a persistent and deeply rooted fear that our public discourse will be drowned out by American voices, that we will somehow lose the thread of the national conversation that is both the method and the measure of any working democracy. From that fear has arisen one of the core missions of Canadian governments in the era of global information: preserving a space for Canadian stories on our own movie, PC and television screens, and on our magazine and book racks.

Keith Spicer, who perhaps more than any other Canadian managed to embody his own maxim during a long career as journalist, academic and chairman of the CRTC, put it this way: "Canada," he once declared, "*is* communications."

The national preoccupation has spawned many larger-than-life personalities. Nineteenth-century newspapermen Joseph Howe and George Brown were early examples, the one passionately opposing Confederation in his *Nova Scotian,* the other advocating it as passionately in the *Globe.* At the turn of the twentieth century, Brandon's Member of Parliament was a man named Clifford Sifton—publisher of the Winnipeg *Free Press.* As Wilfrid Laurier's interior minister, Sifton introduced an Open-the-West policy that brought more than two million people to Canada in the early years of the last century. (Among them were Glaswegians Alexander and Annie Craig and their five children, who settled in Sifton's riding at a place called Virden.) Newspaper owners named Aitken (later Lord Beaverbrook) and Thomson (Lord Thomson of Fleet) combined wealth and social climbing to an extent that the country's reigning contemporary press baron, plain Mr. Conrad Black, can only envy.

Rivalling Black's fortune as the twentieth century ended were those of a recently deceased Quebec separatist, Pierre Peladeau (publishing and printing: $3.8 billion a year), and a quixotic but very much alive

Torontonian named Ted Rogers (cable and cel-phones: $3.7 billion annually). Dwarfing all three moguls and, according to the *Report on Business,* the most profitable corporation in Canada in 1999, was BCE Inc., formerly Bell Canada Enterprises. A telephone company, eh?

Canadians have led the world in the appetite for each new breakthrough in communications. It is not merely that broadcasting—first with radio and then with television—has replaced print as the dominant medium for exchanging information and providing entertainment. The social and political paradigm shift that has occurred is as profound as any produced by steam engines and mass production in an earlier era. From the very first crystal-set radios to satellite TV dishes to the World Wide Web, Canadians have been at the forefront of what demographers and marketers call the "early adopters"—the first kids on their block to acquire each new tool for keeping in touch.

As we pop the cork on a new century, there sometimes seem to be more media than messages. Video images stream ceaselessly from "old-fashioned" off-air television stations, 500-channel satellites sit in space, and microwave towers adorn every tall building and high hill. Through our personal electromagnetic space whiz a clatch of celphone conversations, package-tracking data and directions for muddled taxi drivers. Plugs in the wall connect us to telephone and cable-TV suppliers who bring us not only our best friends but CNN, pay-TV and the Internet. The century that opened to books, newspapers and a smattering of magic-lantern shows closed on all of those plus home entertainment centres, videotape handicams, digital cameras, zip-drives, audio and game CDs, Nintendo cartridges and "smart" cards.

Canadians, predictably, have loved each and every one of them. And even before the advent of the Internet, the first truly revolutionary medium since radio, each evolution in technology has made it more difficult for the businesses that relied on earlier forms of communication to keep their hold on the public's interest.

Broadcasting was not the first viable enterprise to emerge from the harnessing of the electron: telegraphy and telephony might claim those honours. But broadcasting could certainly make a case for being the electronic age's first entirely *novel* industry. (Telephones and telegraphs were merely souped-up versions of older semaphore systems.) Like the Internet at the end of the twentieth century, wireless transmission was at first a technology in search of an industry. Like the Post-it note, it was even mistaken in its early days for an R&D dead-end of sorts: it was handicapped as a competitor to telephony by its inability to preserve the privacy of a conversation. Only when that fault was embraced was the thing turned on its head and the device re-envisioned as one that could reach out across the Canadian expanse—to "broad cast," in fact—to hundreds and thousands of lonely listeners at once, turning them into an *audience*.

But audiences also mean programming. Radio was invented by engineers. To prosper, it had to acquire the know-how of show business.

Broadcasting has never been a trade for the faint of heart. It is inherently risky. Setting up such an endeavour takes an enormous outlay of capital—to buy studios and transmitters, hire "personalities" and front-office staff, acquire program rights—all of it at the front end. Only once a station is up and running is there any prospect that the people out there will actually watch or listen, let alone do so in numbers an advertiser will pay to reach. To a large extent, the costs are the same whether the effort attracts a large audience or a small one.

Even when the audience is a large one, broadcasting is prey, like all other advertising-dependent businesses, to the downturns in everybody *else's* business, as well as to the ebb and flow of fashion among media buyers. Moreover, in the state of constant revolution that is electronics, each fresh investment in new technology is rendered obsolete even before it can be amortized.

One part wiring, one part showbiz and two parts money, broadcasting exists in a state of perpetual tension between its ambitions and their price. In the early days, the dynamic favoured mavericks, risk-takers and one-man shows. The phenomenon was especially strong in the West; Moffat and Craig were only two of the pioneering family names that stood behind the expansion of radio and television in the region. British Columbia had Frank Griffiths, an accountant who turned an obscure New Westminster radio station into a national broadcasting conglomerate: WIC Western International Communications Ltd. Edmonton surgeon Dr. Charles Allard, moonlighting from the operating room, assembled a string of radio and TV stations during the 1970s and '80s. Calgary had H. Gordon Love, who gave the city a second television station in the 1960s, and eccentric cable-meister James R. (now legally "JR"—no periods) Shaw. In Saskatchewan, there were Clifford Sifton's heirs in Regina, and Edward A. Rawlinson and his sons in Prince Albert.

But as the price of the ante rose with the years, most of the pioneers left the table. Many family broadcasters, like the Loves and the Siftons, sold out to larger players. Some fatally fumbled a generational handover (Griffiths's sons lost control of their inheritance within months of his death). Other firms—like those begun by the Shaws and the Moffats—continue as active enterprises managed by descendents of their founders. But much of their ownership has long since passed to market investors, and their executives rule with one eye on how the Street will mark them on each decision.

There have been other consequences of this deep susceptibility to the need for capital. One is the rise of "broadcasters" whose focus is less on show business and wiring than it is on money. As it happens, the same era and neighbourhood that produced Stuart Craig also gave birth to the most successful practitioner of that kind of broadcasting in a generation: Izzy Asper—lawyer, financial analyst, politician, merchant banker and leveraged-buyout artist. While the Craigs spent half a century building a broadcasting system the old-fashioned way, one tower at a time, Asper promoted prospectuses and proxy votes. The war chests he raised enabled him to buy up stations struggling under operators less financially adept than himself (or than the Craigs, for that matter). Ultimately, Asper assembled the most profitable television company in Canada. It happened also to be the one which, among its peers, spent the least of its revenue on producing or acquiring Canadian programs.

In other respects, however, Asper's CanWest Global Communications Corp. shared one salient feature with most of the large television broadcast groups that emerged outside of Quebec in the last quarter of the century. As money came more and more to dominate broadcasting, broadcasting became increasingly centred where the country's money is. Global, the operating arm of Asper's empire—like CTV Inc., CHUM Ltd. and the English service of Canada's national public broadcaster—had its headquarters in Toronto. (The only other large English-language television broadcaster in the country, Griffiths's WIC, did the same until 1999, when its program division moved back to Vancouver; by then, WIC was awaiting break-up, with its television assets likely to end up in Asper's hands.) It implies no disrespect for the professionalism of the Ontarians—most from the same 416 area code—who chose the programs to be exhibited on television screens from Victoria to Pouch Cove to suggest that their viewpoints on the country might suffer from a certain sameness.

But broadcasting is a business unlike other businesses. From the beginning, it was apparent that electronic forms of communication were different from the old modes based on print. In theory, anyone could buy a printing press and a ream of paper and go into publishing. But only so much "spectrum" capable of carrying commercial broadcasting traffic existed. Especially at the outset, when equipment could only be made to work on limited frequency ranges, signals from new broadcasting enterprises often overrode existing transmissions. With no effective referee to allocate frequencies, the result was a cacophony of competing signals where the law of the jungle prevailed: the guy with the biggest transmitter won.

It was just such a development that alarmed Ottawa into creating the country's first agency mandated primarily to regulate broadcasting. When powerful radio stations located in U.S. border cities like Buffalo, New York, and Bellingham, Washington, pointed their antennas north in the late 1920s, Ottawa empanelled a royal commission to investigate. It concluded that, in Canada, "Broadcasting should be on a basis of public service," not private profit. In 1932, Conservative Prime Minister Richard B. Bennett created the Canadian Radio Broadcasting Commission—ancestor of today's CRTC—to see it done.

It quickly became apparent, however, that the Canadian public—at least as represented in Parliament—was not about to foot the bill for a national radio system (nor would it later, for a much more expensive television system). The outcome was a classically Canadian compromise: private players were allowed a role in the national broadcast system, but only if they accepted the ground rules set out by Parliament. Reporting in 1951, a subsequent royal commission under Vincent Massey spelled those rules out when it declared the whole notion that broadcasting in Canada was an "industry" to be "based on a false assumption." Private broadcasters, Massey insisted, had "no civil right to broadcast, or any property rights in broadcasting. They have been granted in the national interest a privilege over their fellow citizens."

To this day, Canada's broadcasters are supposed to reflect that principle of "public service." The law recognizes that turning a profit is necessary—and, for investors, a legitimate goal. But the premise remains that profits should support what the Broadcasting Act terms "the maintenance and enhancement of national identity and cultural sovereignty." Put another way, the greatest benefit that radio and television can provide to the Canadian public is to tell the stories that express who we are and what we care about.

Over the years, however, public benefit has come to be calculated increasingly in dollars and minutes: in the amount of cash or air time invested in "Canadian content." And regulators have raised the "rent" steadily over the years, demanding ever more detailed and expensive commitments in exchange for access to public frequencies. Broadcasters are even subject to a form of quasi-taxation visited upon no other business: Proprietors who wish to transfer their assets by way of sale must demonstrate what the CRTC calls "tangible [public] benefits equal to 10% of the value of the transaction" before the agency will give its green light. Some broadcasters have sought to transform the entire notion of "public benefits" into a sort of commodity system, where credits can be moved around among broadcasting assets like so many trading cards.

Decades of oversight by the Canadian Radio Broadcasting Commission and its successors have created a sort of shadow marketplace to the one in which broadcasters compete for audience and advertising. This parallel market has its own history, language and jurisprudence: "tiers" (what cable service comes in); "twin sticks" (small-market broadcasters who air both CBC and CTV signals from the same tower); the nice distinction between "expectation" and "condition" in a broadcast licence (fulfill the first and earn CRTC bonus points, fail to deliver the second and risk losing a licence).

Politics runs through the process like the proverbial river. By virtue of its mandate, the Canadian Radio-television and Telecommunications Commission cannot hope to escape a good measure of small-p politics. Its job is often to mediate among divergent views of the public good: should it be *this* multilingual channel or *that* all-news one on basic cable? But the commission, after all, is not really an acronym. It is *people*—a panel of ordinary Canadian men and women. Some have had first-hand industry or public policy experience in one of the two broad areas the CRTC regulates: broadcasting and telecommunications. But it is the federal Cabinet that appoints them; and it seldom hurts a prospective commissioner's chances to have a friend on the right side of the Commons. Sometimes the politics that result are closer to the kind New Brunswickers compare to good rum: deep, dark and strong.

It has not been all bad for private broadcasters—or for the public. Far from it. The requirement for a federal licence creates a significant barrier to entry which, over the years, has kept many a lucrative radio and TV market free of pesky competition. The tough questions that commissioners put to those who apply for licences are often good ones. Over the years, CRTC "CanCon"—Canadian content—quotas have demonstrably given the nation's so-called "cultural industries" the start they needed to become global competitors. More important, almost fifty years after Vincent Massey wrote his report, most Canadians still agree with him that the misnamed "airwaves" should be treated as a public asset, rather like an invisible Crown forest that we all have a right to enjoy.

There are corollaries to that principle, though. The first is that the applicant who most deserves the trust of a public broadcasting frequency is not necessarily the richest. Instead, it is he or she who most reflects our Canadian values, who is most dedicated to telling *our* stories, *Canadian* stories—in all of our many accents. The second is that not all of those stories will come out of Toronto.

Some of the stories will come out of a place called the Forks. Once, the patch of floodplain at the confluence of the Red and Assiniboine rivers was a gathering place for generations of Plains Indians who came here each summer to socialize and trade with aboriginals from the northern tundra and the forests to the east. In the early years of Winnipeg's settlement, the Forks became an industrial district. Now, it is in post-industrial recovery under the care of a federal-provincial board of trustees. The trustees are trying to make of it a new kind of meeting ground, a place of playing fields and bars and boutiques, a prairie version of Vancouver's Granville Island or Toronto's Harbourfront. The tallest object around is a huge cement chimney—painted blue.

The fresh paint signals a new presence at the Forks—and in Winnipeg. Behind the chimney is a smallish, boxy building of red brick, not much longer to a side than it is tall, and about three storeys high. "About," because what might be the upper interior storey is instead a huge, steel-plate coal scuttle. Its curved belly descends from the ceiling into a row of offices. They, in turn, overlook a bustling work area hung with lights and populated with desks and computers. On the painted cement floor are strange Xs and Ts of fluorescent tape. Outside, over the glass doors, is a huge letter A.

It stands for "A-Channel." The building is a former steamworks, a heritage structure given new life by the presence of CHMI-TV's long-desired foothold in downtown Winnipeg. The tape on the floor marks camera and announcer positions for live broadcasts from the gleamingly state-of-the art, all-digital news and production centre. For Stuart Craig, A-Channel's presence here marked the end of a twenty-five-year odyssey.

For his three sons, it marks the start of a new campaign.

For nearly half a century, the Craig dynasty's fortunes mirrored those of many another pioneer family of radio and television. But unlike the vast majority of those, the Craigs have not only survived, they have prospered. In the past half-decade, under the new management represented by the third generation of Craigs to run the family business, they have done more than that, breaking out at last from their home province.

In 1996, Craig Broadcast Systems Inc., the successor to Western Manitoba Broadcasters, startled the business press by applying to bring a fourth television service to Alberta. Its only rival for the licence was Izzy Asper's CanWest Global Communications. CanWest Global has half the life history of Craig Broadcast. It also has about ten times Craig's annual revenues, and a thousand times its public profile. None of the pundits even saw a contest.

The Craigs were used to that. They have been dismissed before. In one especially tasteless moment, the *Globe and Mail* once alluded to them as "yokels." At CRTC hearings, rivals routinely question whether some unheard-of father-and-sons broadcast shop from little Brandon is *really* up to the financial and management tests of a major market.

Guess who won.

Alberta got its first new television station in more than twenty years when A-Channel went on the air in Edmonton and Calgary in September 1997. Two years later, MTN was reborn and rebranded, with a long-sought home of its own in Winnipeg and a new name: "A-Channel Manitoba."

"The letter 'A'," enthuses Drew Craig, "means being the best, being number one!"

After fifty years in the game, Craig Broadcast is demanding the right to play at centre ice. In the same week that the new studio opened at the Forks, Craig applied to bring A-Channel to British Columbia. If that application is successful, it may not be long before the giant A is lighting up TV screens in the heartland of southern Ontario. "Our ambition," Stuart Craig candidly revealed, "is to set up a national network."

Any city slicker inclined to crack a smile should first check the rules that govern broadcasting in this country—and then weigh the record of how the Craigs have done so far.

2

Pioneers

It's tempting to imagine the ghost of one expatriate Italian explorer looking over the shoulder of another very much alive at the dawn of the century just passed. The month was December 1901. The place: a small, panelled room in an unheated stone tower on a windswept hill overlooking St. John's, Newfoundland, the eastern gatepost of the continent. Mariners have sought shelter here, their anxious eyes probing fog and spray for the narrow entrance amid terrifying cliffs, at least since Giovanni Caboto (known to his English employers as John Cabot) recorded his landing in 1497. Now Guglielmo Marconi was camped out in the newly erected tower—named after Cabot and completed only a year earlier—on a voyage of discovery in a different realm.

Building on earlier work by André Marie Ampère, Heinrich Hertz and James Clerk Maxwell, Marconi had already shown that not only could invisible electromagnetic rays be described as a real force, but they could be made to carry messages using the same dot-dash code employed by telegraphers. Unappreciated in Italy, Marconi—like Caboto—had found backers in Britain, whose battleships began testing his "radio" equipment over short distances in 1899. But Marconi wanted to prove radio's potential against a more serious challenge: he was determined to show it could send a message across the Atlantic Ocean.

To that end, he had built a transmitter facility in Poldhu, Cornwall, and a receiver station near Cape Cod, in Massachusetts. He planned to perform his demonstration during the winter, since cold weather seemed to favour the passage of electromagnetic waves through the atmosphere. But November brought wicked gales along the stormy Gulf of Maine, and a particularly fierce blast destroyed Marconi's receiving station at South Wellfleet. He fell back to an alternative site: Signal Hill near St. John's.

Outside, in the bitter midday cold, assistants manhandled the ground lines of a large kite held aloft by the powerful wind off the Atlantic.

Beneath it trailed the receiving antenna for Marconi's apparatus. (Short of time and money to erect new antenna towers, the inventor had found Signal Hill's near-constant winds as much of an attraction is its proximity to Cornwall; the Newfoundland tower was now some 1,280 kilometres closer than Wellfleet had been.) On the far side of the Atlantic, associates at Marconi's Poldhu base had instructions to transmit a single letter of the Morse alphabet continuously between 3:00 and 6:00 p.m. over several days. On the first day, the wind at Signal Hill was so strong it carried away the kite. But on Thursday, December 12, as Marconi huddled in his overcoat against the chill of Cabot's drafty tower, clutching a primitive earpiece to his head, he heard it, faint but distinct against the static crackle and hiss: the three small "clicks" of the Morse letter S. The experiment succeeded again on the following day, and on Saturday, December 14, Marconi issued a statement announcing his achievement to the world.

We forget how little time has passed since Marconi first demonstrated the infant technology from which so many now-familiar applications descend. More than any other discovery, it was radio (and its offshoot, television) that led the way in reducing data to electronic impulses—at first in analogue and later in digital forms—and in developing ever more sophisticated means for that data's manipulation and dissemination. In the hundred years since Marconi's crude experiments, electromagnetic radio waves have been harnessed in literally countless ways, applied to everything from radar-guided missiles to CAT scanners to radio-controlled model cars. No other technology, with the possible exception of the internal combustion engine, had a greater influence on the century just passed—not even computers, which were themselves made possible by the existence of tubes and transistors initially developed for broadcast electronics. Whatever else it may have been, the twentieth century was unquestionably the century of radio.

The information age just over the horizon was far from apparent to Marconi's contemporaries. In 1901, it was still very much a material world. The overwhelming majority of jobs, whether in resources or manufacturing, dealt in goods, often under physically demanding, dirty and dangerous circumstances. Wealth, a matter of hard capital, real estate and cash (backed, always, by gold), was concentrated in the hands of very few.

Even so, change was in the air. The flowering of invention seemed to prefigure the sweeping social re-engineering to come. Alexander

Graham Bell's telephone was already a quarter-century old in December of 1901; Edison's lightbulb was twenty-two. Twenty-four months later, on a North Carolina beach, two brothers from Dayton, Ohio, would make humankind's first powered flight, covering 259 metres of sand. Political debate bubbled with seditious notions about capitalism and communism, utopias of different stripes, and whether females could be trusted with the ballot. Millions of men and women were meanwhile voting with their feet, breaking ties with overcrowded Europe and betting their future on the "New World."

In Ottawa, Prime Minister Wilfrid Laurier was at the height of his power. Then in the second year of his second term, the Liberal leader was eager to advance Canada's independence—as much from the British Empire as from the increasingly powerful colossus to the south. Hearing about Marconi's success in Newfoundland (which would of course not become part of Canada for another forty-eight years), Laurier understood the significance of the Italian's discovery. He dispatched an aide to intercept the inventor at Sydney, Nova Scotia, on his way back to the United States, and to make him an offer. In the deal that ensued, the Dominion government paid Marconi an initial subsidy of $80,000. In return, Marconi rebuilt his base station for trans-Atlantic radio experiments in Glace Bay, Nova Scotia, and later opened a laboratory in Montreal.

Clifford Sifton, Laurier's minister of the interior and the Member of Parliament from Brandon, wanted to be sure that Canada attracted its fair share of the masses abandoning the old world for the new. Under Sifton's direction, Canadian officials actively promoted the country as a destination for immigrants from Europe, offering two powerful attractions. One was free land in the Canadian West: a quarter-section to any settler who undertook to break and improve it. The other was Sifton's policy that, wherever possible, immigrants from the same home country would receive land grants near each other, a system that provided for what today would be called ready-made support networks.

Intent on leveraging the national policy, many communities in the West undertook their own promotion campaigns. Brandon's civic authorities published a series of brochures describing the region's potential in glowing terms and had these distributed in Europe to would-be immigrants. "No country offers better advantages to the capitalist for the investment of his surplus funds," read one, adding in typically purple fashion: "But to the enterprising poor man above all others the Great Canadian North-West is in the fullest sense of the term, the 'Great Land of Promise.'"

Brandon had some reason for its boisterous optimism. Manitoba's second-largest settlement had sprung from open prairie over the course of a single summer in 1881, after an engineer working for the Canadian Pacific Railway selected the sleepy bend in the Assiniboine River west of Winnipeg as a divisional point where trains would be broken up and reassembled. Within months, a tent city dotted the flatland by the river. By that autumn, Brandon boasted a hotel, three stores and a billiard hall. It would eventually become a major crossroads for rail lines running in all directions, for the Northern Pacific and Great North West Central in addition to the CPR. By 1906, its population had grown to more than 10,000.

That year also witnessed more milestones in radio. Since Marconi's trans-Atlantic demonstration, wireless telegraphy—Morse code over the air—had found one early application as a means for ships at sea to communicate with shore and with each other. In Canada, as a consequence, authority over the new technology was given to the federal Department of Marine.

In other respects, radio remained an experimental curiosity. Still, the race to develop the new technology was fierce and increasingly well-funded by large corporate backers. These included U.S.-based giants like General Electric and AT&T, as well as dozens of small workshops operated by visionary entrepreneurs. Among the latter was Reginald Fessenden, a Canadian engineer who had worked with both Thomas Edison and George Westinghouse before setting out on his own earlier in the decade. One of Marconi's closest rivals, Fessenden successfully transmitted and received brief voice messages between stations in Machrihanish, Scotland, and Brant Rock, Massachusetts, early in 1906. Then, on Christmas eve of that year, Fessenden startled wireless operators on a number of vessels at sea off New England when he transmitted the first-ever public broadcast of music and voice. The "program" included a seasonal message from Fessenden, a phonograph recording of Handel's *Largo,* and the engineer himself performing *Silent Night* on his violin.

It seems certain that sometime during the year that followed, one or another of the inducements that Sifton and his officials were offering for settlement in Canada reached the ears of two Scottish families for whom the old country held diminishing prospects. What is certain is that early in 1908—according to family lore, on the same day—two ships pulled away from their Clydeside piers, each carrying hundreds of hopeful passengers bidding good-bye to homes and families in search of a better life in Canada.

On board one vessel was Alex Craig, a casket-maker and undertaker from Howood, a suburb of Glasgow, along with his wife, Annie, and their five children: Tom, the eldest, Mary, Elizabeth, John Boyd (named after his mother's family) and little Anne. On the other ship were Andrew Middleton, a clerk from Edinburgh, his wife, Mary, and their three children: Mary, Andrew and Catherine. Andrew Middleton and his family eventually settled in Brandon; Alex and Annie Craig and their brood, after a stop in Toronto, made it about 80 kilometres further west, to Virden, Mantoba, before putting down stakes.

Over the next decade, both families established themselves in their new country. Andrew Middleton found work as the manager of a fruit and grocery warehouse, but he was to struggle financially throughout his life; the family lived in a series of rented apartments and houses. Alex Craig, an inventive man who was good with his mind as well as his hands (his home back in Howood had boasted light from a gas generator he had designed and built himself), had modestly more success. His small dairy acreage didn't make the family rich, but it did provide enough cash and garden produce to keep everyone clothed and fed.

"I learned about hard work before I was out of school," John Craig would say later about his childhood. Days started early with the need to milk half a dozen cows by hand. In winter, they ended early as well: meals were served at 4:00, to be eaten before dark fell and the only light came from coal-oil lamps. (Electricity would not reach much of rural Manitoba until the late 1930s.) Elizabeth and young John drove the buggy—in winter, a sleigh—to deliver fresh milk to customers in Virden. All the kids from both families entered and completed public school. The Scots immigrants were becoming Canadians.

The technologies of the new century were establishing themselves as well. In 1908, Henry Ford began turning out the first of some 8 million Model T's—cars destined to democratize the automobile even while Ford's mass-production technique revolutionized manufacturing. The following year, newsreels appeared in movie houses. And in early 1912, an event occurred which, amid tragedy, would dramatically illustrate the power of radio. That spring, the great White Star liner *Titanic*, the largest passenger ship built to the time, struck an iceberg on the fifth day of its maiden voyage and sank; 1,522 people drowned, but the vessel's SOS message, sent over the *Titanic*'s state-of-the-art radio in Morse code, brought several other ships to the scene of the disaster in time to rescue nearly 700 others. Wireless also carried the first reports of the "unsinkable" vessel's fate to an astonished world.

The following year, Canada amended its eight-year-old Radiotelegraph Act. Among other things, the new rules required all passenger ships calling at Canadian ports to carry a radio and a qualified operator on board.

Interest in radio had begun to spread beyond the world of scientific and commercial researchers. Helped by instructions in magazines like *Popular Mechanics* and *Science Illustrated,* showing how to make "crystal-set" radio receivers out of inexpensive components, technically minded young people embraced radio with the same passion and enthusiasm that a later generation of hackers would display for computers and the Internet. In 1911, the Department of Marine's Radio Branch in Ottawa issued its first "experimental" radio station licence to Frank Vaughan, a young New Brunswicker who belonged to a family of shipbuilders and ships' captains. The next year, an Ontario tire company and an explosives maker in British Columbia with operations in Howe Sound, near Vancouver, applied for commercial radio licences to communicate between their different locations.

Two considerations still held radio back from wider use. One was the fact that equipment based on the designs of Fessenden and others, which could broadcast a continuous signal carrying voice or music, required that a continuous supply of voltage be delivered to a transmitter. With the electronics of the day, this remained difficult. As a result, all radio traffic—mainly marine communications—was conducted in dot-dash codes. Fascinating stuff to a handful of enthusiasts like Vaughan, perhaps, but hardly the key to mass appeal. Even so, Ottawa issued another sixteen private commercial radio licences in 1914, including one to the Marconi Wireless Telegraph Co.'s laboratory in Montreal; it was assigned the call letters XWA.

Then, in August of that year, war came to Europe, and the ties to Empire that Laurier had sought to loosen were eagerly taken up by his successor. Conservative Prime Minister Robert Borden promised that Canada would support Britain's war with an army of 500,000 men—

from a population at the time of barely 8 million. War dropped Canadian society into a vortex of Imperial propaganda, bitter domestic division over compulsory military service, and social change, as women took over many of the jobs left behind by men serving at the front. With the nation's energies focussed on the war effort, private-sector development in radio was frozen. Research came under the direction—and veil—of military exigency.

The war's end in 1918 found a world transformed. The 60,000 Canadian lives lost on Europe's battlefields, paradoxically, had helped forge a sense of national pride even while straining national unity. Canadian women—some of whom had won the temporary right to vote on behalf of absent husbands in uniform, and many more of whom had felt for the first time the thrill of a pay cheque—would refuse to return politely to their traditional places in the home. A large body of demobilized troops brought back not only pent-up appetites for the freedom, pleasures and opportunity of civvy street, but also technical skills acquired in the service. Businesses began to seek out civilian markets for advances in technology achieved during the years of conflict, especially in the fields of aviation and wireless communications.

In Manitoba, John Boyd Craig turned seventeen in 1918. At 5 feet, 5 inches or so, he was no giant, but he held himself with the cocky swagger of a young bantam rooster. The Scots burr of his childhood had faded with time, and his easy manner and sharp, inquisitive mind helped the young man win friends easily. In the quintessentially Canadian game of hockey, he excelled behind the crease. The year the war in Europe ended, John Boyd tended goal for the Virden senior hockey team—a vocation that was to prove his stepping-stone to a career in radio. After a brief stint behind the counter of a hardware store, he followed older brother Tom (who would eventually rise to a vice-president's position at the Royal) into banking. The Canadian Imperial Bank of Commerce started John at the bank's Virden branch, then moved him to Kelvington, Saskatchewan.

The next few years were to prove pivotal both for radio and for John Craig. The war had seen most of the technical hurdles to reliable radio broadcast and reception overcome. But patent rights to several key technologies remained in the hands of separate—and competing—corporations. Armistice in Europe brought an end to a patent truce that had prevailed among the warring rights-holders so long as the top national priority was defeating the enemy. In 1919, however, the U.S.

navy, backed by the weight of the Wilson administration, brokered a deal among the most important patent holders, including American Marconi, the Radio Corporation of America (RCA, a General Electric subsidiary) and AT&T, to pool their radio patents. The arrangement cleared the way for manufacturers to produce radio transmitters and receivers in large numbers—if demand for them ever developed. How that might come about was still not clear. As would be the case again seventy-five years later with the World Wide Web at its inception, the powerful new capabilities of radio were all medium, no message.

But this would soon change. The Marconi lab in Montreal had been one of the very few pursuing continuous voice transmission—as opposed to dot-dash code—over radio. Late in 1919, it began experimenting with test broadcasts under a new identity: the federal Radio Branch had retired the company's former XWA designation and replaced it with the letters CFCF. (The call sign, the oldest still in use in Canada, now belongs to a Montreal radio and TV station.)

In May 1920, the Marconi lab mounted an unprecedented demonstration of radio's potential. In what was likely the world's first scheduled public radio broadcast, CFCF transmitted a special program of live music and short addresses to coincide with a meeting of the Royal Society of Canada, an assembly of the nation's most respected scientists and academics. The signal from Montreal came in clearly to a receiver and loudspeakers set up 192 kilometres away in Ottawa, where a VIP audience included both Prime Minister Borden and Opposition Leader William Lyon Mackenzie King.

Over the following months, Marconi acquired licences and put on demonstration broadcasts in Vancouver and Toronto (where CHCB did the world's first remote broadcast from the Canadian National Exhibition). In December of that year, CFCF began regular (though not yet daily) scheduled broadcasts. It was the second station in the world to do so. The Westinghouse lab in Pittsburgh had received a radio licence from American authorities in late October, and its station KDKA began scheduled broadcasts on November 2 with a report on Republican Warren Harding's defeat of Democrat James Cox in that day's presidential election.

Both stations adopted practices that would come to define the essence of commercial radio. The very earliest voice broadcasts had consisted of nothing more than engineers endlessly repeating test phrases or the numbers from one to ten. Tiring of that, experimenters began setting up phonographs beside their microphones and broadcasting the reproduced music. Both CFCF and KDKA soon began mentioning on the air the names of the music stores that had supplied the recordings. The chemistry of music and advertising would fuel radio's commercial success for generations to come.

Fate, meanwhile, was moving John Boyd Craig closer to the revolutionary new medium. In 1925, the talented young netminder accepted an offer from the Brandon Wheat Kings, a Senior A league team, to come and play in the larger centre. Quitting his bank career—for which he had never, in truth, felt much appetite—the enterprising farm boy soon found work at a local automobile sales and service establishment. Self-confident, always snappily dressed and with a quick-witted charm, Johnny Craig helped land an especially lucrative contract, delivering a fleet of garbage trucks and wagons to the Brandon public works department. In short order, Craig was a partner in McCreary Motors, which, in addition to Hudson and Whippet automobiles, sold furnaces, appliances . . . and radios.

The last were becoming especially hot items. Heavily promoted by manufacturers and supported by a growing number of broadcasting stations, the "radio craze," as commentators of the day called it, took off. By April 1922, there were 21 licensed radio stations in Canada—four of them in Winnipeg—and 2,588 receivers. Licences were required for these as well—and would be well into the 1950s, at prices of between one and three dollars a year. By the following year, the number of licensed listeners had more than tripled to 9,954. The Canadian National Railroad established stations in several cities—the country's first primitive broadcast network—and installed receivers and earphones in the club cars of its trains. Newspapers—many of whose owners had acquired radio licences—launched regular features on the subject in their entertainment sections. Magazines sprang up, dedicated to the growing market of radio fans.

In 1925, one of radio's last technical shortcomings was resolved. Until then, both broadcast and receiving equipment worked only on direct current—the kind obtained from batteries. That limited the duration of broadcasts to the lifetime of the batteries being used. At the midpoint of the 1920s, however, Rogers Batteryless, a Toronto company, introduced the first radios that operated on alternating current. (Two years later, the company would launch Toronto station CFRB in order to help sell its receiving equipment.) The new generation of radios also sounded better and could be equipped with loudspeakers so that everyone in the room—not just those with earphones—could hear the program. At about $325, though, a top-of-the-line model was still beyond the reach of most consumers; even a plainer set, at $175, was pricey.

Radio was finally closing in on Brandon. In 1923, after all four of the commercial stations launched the previous year in Winnipeg had shut down, the Manitoba government, through the provincial telephone company, put station CKY on the air in the capital. Its most popular service was cattle and grain price reports, which gave listeners on farms within transmission range hitherto unavailable market data for the commodities they produced. By 1927, farmers in the province's southwest were demanding a similar service, and the powerful James Richardson and Sons grain-brokerage house in Winnipeg seemed ready to provide it: the company applied to the Radio Branch for a licence to put a radio station in the basement of its Brandon office.

The application was turned down. Instead, federal officials gave the Manitoba Telephone System permission the following year to open a radio station in Brandon—using a hand-me-down transmitter that would become available when CKY acquired new and more powerful gear.

Nineteen twenty-seven had begun badly for John Craig. Midway through his third season in the net for the Wheat Kings, a slapshot struck him in the chest and broke his breastbone. While still convalescing from that injury, Craig came down with scarlet fever and was hospitalized with dozens of other victims of the national epidemic in a sanitarium just north of the city. His illness proved not such a bad thing, however, when Craig's girlfriend of the time came visiting—and brought with her a pretty, effervescent chum named Catherine Middleton. Shortly after his release from hospital, John Boyd became engaged to the personable Middleton, who worked as a stenographer.

A year of big decisions for the young car salesman followed. John Craig determined early in 1928 to shed his partnership in McCreary Motors and set up on his own. Forming Craig Motors Ltd., he bought a British American Oil Co. gasoline franchise and opened for business in a meticulously whitewashed building at the corner of 10th Street and Louise Avenue in Brandon. (The site is now occupied by a new city hall, opened in 1970.) On September 1, 1928, John and Catherine were wed and moved into a stucco and brick bungalow a dozen blocks from the business, on 22nd Street.

On December 1, 1928, CKX Brandon took to the air. Amid heated local controversy, the Manitoba Telephone System had persuaded Brandon city council to help foot the bill for the new station. As a result, CKX's two antenna towers—cross-braced self-supporting pylons reminiscent of the Eiffel Tower—stood on the east lawn of Brandon's city hall. The first broadcast was a musical variety program featuring several soloists and such hits of the day as "If You Want the Rainbow You Must Have the Rain." Those who didn't possess radio sets of their own were invited to St. Paul's United Church, where a receiver and loudspeaker were set up, and the broadcast, according to accounts of the day, was "heard to advantage."

Eleven months later, on October 29, 1929, the stock market collapsed. Wheat prices, already dropping, went into freefall. The first chill winds of the decade-long economic downturn that would earn the title "the Great Depression" had blown in. The Prairies would be among the regions hardest hit, and neither Brandon nor the newlywed Craigs would escape. Somewhat paradoxically, it would also prove a golden decade for radio.

First, the price of radios dropped sharply. By 1930, models that had commanded $300 three years earlier could be had for under $60. Once a radio was purchased, moreover, the programs it received were essentially free, although the federal government continued to collect a $1-a-year licence fee throughout the Depression. For cash-strapped families forced to pinch every penny, that made radio just about the cheapest form of entertainment around. Nowhere was this more true than in the rural households of the Prairies, where alternatives in the form of live performances or even movie houses were rare. As it happened, the flat terrain of the West also favoured the propagation of radio signals giving prairie residents some of the widest choices of programs anywhere. It was not unusual for avid listeners to pick up stations from as far away as Toronto, Ontario, and Victoria, B.C., on the same evening.

But the economic chill continued to deepen. In the West, drought added its misery to low grain prices. By 1933, one Canadian in five was unemployed. In Saskatchewan, one family in three was on the dole. On June 3 of that year, in the very depths of the Great Depression, John and Catherine Craig had a son. Andrew Stuart Craig would afterward remember that his father always seemed to be working—even on Sunday afternoons after church, when John Boyd would pump gas and wash windshields to save the cost of hiring an extra man. For a time, the family would be forced to have their telephone removed as an economy measure. But the radio, a velvet-toned DeForest model in a wood cabinet, "was on all day long," Stuart recalled. "It was an important part of the household."

Throughout the decade, the choice and extent of radio programming continued to improve. Locally, programs had been intermittent: CKX, like many other stations, at first broadcast only three evenings a week. By the year of Stuart Craig's birth, the schedule was daily—for about an hour at lunch and two or three hours at night. Grain and livestock prices still captured farm audiences, but everyone could relate to musical variety programs such as *The Imperial Oil Hour of Fine Music* and *The Eveready Hour.* Comedy shows like *Amos 'n' Andy* and mystery serials like *The Eno Crime Club* made their appearance, as did live broadcasts from sporting events.

In 1932, the Conservative government of R. B. Bennett created the Canadian Radio Broadcasting Commission with a mandate to establish a national radio network. The commission, through contracts with outside producers, soon began to turn out distinctly Canadian radio fare, which often scored well with audiences. But attempts to create a strong national network of public broadcasting stations floundered, in part because of feuding among the three commissioners. In 1936, the CRBC collapsed in a scandal of its own making: in the election the previous fall, it had helped to produce flagrantly partisan political broadcasts favouring the Conservatives—who lost. The commission was replaced by the Canadian Broadcasting Corporation.

By then, CKX Brandon was broadcasting daily from dawn to midnight. Its fare was a combination of local productions, network programming from the CBC and popular American shows.

Craig Sr. was soon to get a first-hand taste of the new medium's potential. A natural salesman, he sought to supplement the income from his garage by acting as CKX's part-time commercial manager. In the fall of 1938, inspired by Foster Hewitt's live play-by-play broadcasts from Maple Leaf Gardens, Craig succeeded in selling sponsorship for a Brandon Wheat Kings game. It was a bold move that promised to attract a wide audience. But there was one small catch. As Humphrey Davies, the station's transmitter operator, recalled later in an unpublished memoir: "Who would do the play-by-play description?" The answer: "The only staff member with any hockey experience—former goalkeeper, Johnny Craig."

But if things on the Canadian Prairies were looking up at last by the end of the thirties, war was again in the air in Europe. In the same year Stuart Craig entered the world, Hitler was named chancellor of Germany. When Hitler's armies invaded Poland on September 1, 1939, Britain and France promptly declared war. Canada's declaration followed a week later. Radio stations across the country, CKX among them, were ordered onto twenty-four-hour standby to be ready to carry war bulletins at a moment's notice. Brandon's Prince Edward Hotel, the city's finest (long since demolished), contributed a cot for the CKX staff member keeping watch overnight.

It did not take long for Ottawa to impose rationing on gasoline and tires, or for Canadian car makers to shut down civilian production lines in favour of military orders. In one stroke, Craig Motors Ltd. lost its three main business lines. Early in 1940, determined to preserve his good credit and personal reputation, Johnny Boyd swallowed hard and closed the doors of his company for the duration of the war.

3

Betting on Air

John Boyd Craig would not go to war. It wasn't reluctance: a military doctor found a previously undetected flaw in Craig's heart, and the former hockey player was deemed unfit for military service. Instead, he would put his considerable energies into the war effort on the home front.

For the first year, he found work managing the Red Cross office in Winnipeg. But that meant a weekly commute from Brandon, and leaving Catherine on her own with an active seven-year-old. By the time the United States entered the conflict on December 7, 1941—after the Japanese attacked its Pacific fleet in Pearl Harbor—Craig was back in Brandon, managing Victory Bond drives.

It was a perfect mission for the gregarious and well-liked Johnny Craig. In a profile, the Brandon *Sun* described the Scots immigrant as a "controlled dynamo [who] is utterly fearless when faced with hard work. In business details his mind works like a rapid calculating machine. Men in groups watch John in action."

Energetic, insightful and full of laughter, John Craig seemed to carry bonhomie around him like a cologne. "It was always a pleasant visit when I went to see John," recalls Deputy Speaker of the Senate Gildas Molgat, a Manitoba business consultant who got to know Craig when the latter became active in the Liberal Party. "He was a very direct, very good-humoured man, always smiling."

And Craig was inventive. To dramatize the need to support the war-bond drive, he conceived and organized a "What If Germany Won?" day in Brandon. A thousand Canadian soldiers from nearby Base Shilo donned captured German uniforms and goose-stepped down the city's main street accompanied by Wehrmacht tanks and half-tracks and swastika flags; some handed out German money. It made a deep impression, and Brandonites dug a little deeper.

On another occasion, Craig called upon his old contacts in radio, as well as his new ones in the local military establishment. Brandon at the time was home to the Commonwealth Air Training Plan. Through the plan's hangars passed thousands of young men from Britain, Australia, New Zealand and even the United States before that country joined the war, as well as Canadians. The raw recruits were able to pick up at least the basics of flying and flight service in the safety of western Manitoba, before being flung into battle in Europe and elsewhere. A bright yellow Bristol Bomber still stands alongside the Trans-Canada Highway at Brandon, advertising the presence of a museum dedicated to the plan.

John Craig talked base commanders into contributing another type of trainer, an Anson bomber, to his scheme. Enlisting mechanics from No. 12 Flying Training School and engineers from CKX, he had two 2-metre-long loudspeakers installed in the belly of the flying beast, and radio equipment wired in to put the bomber in two-way communication with a Royal Canadian Air Force mobile ground unit, the CKX studio and Victory Bond fund headquarters. On the day of the drive, as bonds were sold, the climbing totals of money raised were announced simultaneously over the radio and from the loudspeakers blaring from beneath the Anson, as it flew slowly at low altitude over rural communities throughout the district.

As the prairie snow began to melt in the spring of 1945, victory in Europe seemed certain at last. Japan was in retreat in the Pacific. It was possible to hope for a return to a normal civilian life. The Craig family had had a better war than many, but the little stucco-and-brick bungalow on 22nd Street was becoming cramped. In 1940, Catherine's parents, Andrew and Mary Middleton, had exhausted their savings and come to live with the Craigs. Andrew soon passed away, but for most of the next decade Stuart would share the bungalow's small finished basement with his Scots grandmother. In May 1944, eleven years after Stuart's birth, the family expanded again when Catherine bore a baby daughter who received her mother's name.

With peace in the air, John Craig put out feelers among former associates in the car business. All the manufacturers were tooling up for a return to building civilian models, and there was no question there was a market: Canadians hadn't been able to buy new cars in six years. The Nash company seemed likely to be faster off the mark than Ford or General Motors. Scraping together what he had saved from the closure of his pre-war service station and a little money put aside from his salary as bond-drive manager, Craig acquired the rights to Nash models for western Manitoba. Japan's surrender on August 15, 1945, marked the final defeat of the Axis powers. Early the following year, Craig Motors reopened for business.

The company prospered. Nash did indeed get the jump on other car makers, and for a period of time in 1946 and 1947, it was the only new car the eager buyers of Brandon could get their hands on. As the vehicles arrived, four or five cars a month, Craig would consult a list he kept in his office desk and dole them out, scrupulously following the order in which customers had placed their deposits with him. "He did very well," recalled Stuart in later years. He could have done even better. Impatience for new wheels was running so strong that numerous customers tried to negotiate their way past those ahead of them on the list with the aid of a little cash. It wasn't unusual for a buyer to offer as much as $500 extra for early delivery of an $1,800 to $2,000 Nash. "His profit could have doubled easily," Stuart stated matter-of-factly. "One guy even threatened him." But it made no difference: Johnny Craig was a man of his word, and you got your car when your name came up.

"He liked a fair business, he liked a clean business," Stuart said later of his father. "The customer always came first for Dad." There were values, time would make clear, that were bred deep in the family bone.

The Craigs, then as now, were far from pious. They attended services most Sundays at St. Paul's United Church, but Johnny liked a drink of rye and was no stranger to the salty language of the locker room—or the newsroom. He and Catherine knew how to have fun and enjoyed a wide circle of friends. But along with a sense of fair play, John Craig strove to pass on to his son and daughter the complementary Scots virtues of hard work, thrift and, for all his showmanship, personal modesty. Most of the socializing John and Catherine did was unpretentious—dinners or parties at home or at their friends' homes. And the son of the Glasgow undertaker made no distinction based on another person's class, wealth or colour. At a time when anti-aboriginal racism was widely acceptable, John often drove young Stuart to meet pals from the area's "Indian school." Remembers Stu's sister, Catherine Craig Moffat (her husband is no relation to Randall): "I was taught you should appreciate what you have, and not always ask for a lot of things."

But if John Craig was doing well from the brisk sales of Nash cars in the post-war euphoria, in late 1947 it seemed that his ship was really about to come in. Craig Motors won the rights to distribute General Motors' Pontiac and Buick products throughout western Manitoba, as soon as the first vehicles rolled off the assembly lines in Detroit the following year. Forget Roy Thomson's claim for that television was "a licence to print money." In the late 1940s and early 1950s, with a literal army of returning servicemen looking for transport and a national fleet of worn-out civilian vehicles in need of replacement, no more gold-plated profit-making prospect existed anywhere in Canada than that of a GM dealership.

Craig would turn it down.

When fate intervened, it came in the form of a classic Canadian federal-provincial constitutional tussle.

In 1945, the province of Quebec passed its own Broadcasting Act, authorizing the creation of a provincial broadcasting service. But more than a decade earlier, the British House of Lords had ruled that the federal government had exclusive jurisdiction over radio communications. On May 3, 1946, responding to the Quebec initiative, Ottawa announced that no broadcasting licences would be issued to "other governments or corporations owned by other governments." Any provinces that owned radio stations had to get rid of them. In December 1947, Manitoba Premier Stuart Garson took to the air to tell Manitobans that both CKY and CKX were on the block. The CBC had put in a reserve bid for CKY, but the Brandon station was still unspoken for.

Calling on his wide circle of contacts in the town's business community, John Craig began rounding up investors. In the end, fifty-three men and women allowed themselves to be recruited as shareholders in the venture, and on April 1, 1948, the Manitoba Telephone System transferred the licence for CKX Radio to Western Manitoba Broadcasters Ltd. of Brandon. The price: $65,000.

A Brandon physician, Dr. H. O. McDiarmid, would be the company's founding president. John Craig would be managing director. Of 5,900 WestMan shares issued, Craig held the largest number, just over 2,000. Seven other people had stakes of a few hundred shares. But most of the investors were in for only small amounts: ten shares apiece. Craig's block amounted to a commanding 34 per cent, but it was no guarantee of control, a shortfall that would come back to haunt the family in the decades to come.

For the moment, though, the newly formed company had more

pressing concerns. CKX had acquired new studios during the war. A small red-brick building with decorative Art Deco touches to its exterior and the Manitoba Telephone System logo in coloured mosaic on the front-office floor now stood in the shadow of Brandon city hall. The station's antenna towers had been removed from the civic front lawn to a new location across the river, just below the mental hospital that occupied the bluffs north of the Assiniboine.

The war years had cemented Canadians' relationship to radio. With the lives of loved ones often on the line, it became a national habit to tune in at 9:00 p.m. for the evening news, where the battles raging half a world away could frequently be heard beneath the measured tones of reporters. Those reports were often far more graphic than the ones broadcast on U.S. stations; American reporters were not allowed as close to the battle front as the Canadians were.

By 1948, CKX's broadcast day ran from six in the morning until midnight, later on Saturday night, and the station carried popular imported American shows and Canadian fare distributed on the CBC's Dominion network. The line-up in prime time included *Fibber McGee and Molly* and the *Fred Allen Show* from the States and *The Happy Gang*, produced in Toronto, as well as mystery series and every major sports championship. Twenty-three people worked for the station, from manager on down to transmitter attendant. But the operation was losing money.

The numbers were bad on both sides of the balance sheet. National advertising revenue was negligible: that income went to the network, which paid paltry fees for the air time it took up on CKX. The station was living on the local advertising that Brandon—still a community of only 20,000 people—and the smaller towns and hamlets of southwestern Manitoba could support. And it was paying the salaries of twenty-three people. John let half a dozen of them go and doubled the sales staff, to two. By the end of his first full year in charge of CKX, Craig was able to report to his investors that Western Manitoba Broadcasters had brought in nearly $100,000 during 1949—and turned a 20 per cent net profit.

It was a gratifying turn-around. But in fact, there was hardly any excuse *not* to do well in the years on either side of the twentieth century's high noon.

On the global stage, there were tensions. The Cold War got icy in Berlin, then hot in Korea. But the conflict in Asia was contained, and by the time it ended in 1953 the number of Canadian casualties—312 soldiers, airmen and sailors—while sobering, seemed small in comparison to the conflagration just past. The menace of the A- and H-bombs, happily, remained just that; for all the jitters, the Big One never did drop. And the ideological excesses of McCarthyism, for the most part, stayed south of the border.

Politics aside, the nation's economic life was good. Good? It had never been better. An Allied conference at Bretton Woods in the second-last year of the war had laid the ground rules for a new World Bank, and a general trading agreement had followed in 1948. Canadian exports soared. And so did the number of Canadians. Demand for cars wasn't the only domestic desire that had been pent up during six years of war. By 1957, there were 40 per cent more Canadians than there had been at war's end, thanks to the baby boom. Canada's gross domestic product would increase nearly as fast, roaring ahead at double-digit annual rates in four of the five years between 1947 and 1952. Canada was even expanding geographically: in 1949, Newfoundland joined Confederation.

It was a time when the whole continent seemed to be throwing out the last holdovers from the Depression and getting into the spirit of the modern age. Ottawa was talking about a new national project: a Trans-Canada Highway to do for rubber wheels what the CPR had done for steel. In Brandon, city politicians voted to close down the municipal horse barns and pave more of the streets.

For the two Craig children, it was also a golden time. Stuart was enough older than Catherine that sibling rivalry was not an issue; he willingly amused his kid sister for hours on end with card games, wearing the surface clean off the table the two used in the bungalow's kitchen. Both remember their family life as loving and joyful, if not indulgent, the house frequently throbbing with music and conversation as their parents entertained friends. Johnny Craig's one great luxury was a few weeks each summer with the family at a rented cabin in the aspen woods that fringe Clear Lake in Riding Mountain National Park, a dusty hour-and-a-half's drive over gravel roads north of Brandon.

It did not take long for the broadcasting bug to bury itself deep in young Stuart's psyche. Not quite fifteen when WestMan took over CKX, he soon became a fixture in the red-brick building beside city hall. "I loved radio," he recalled. "I'd hang around the control room. I got to know all the announcers." Soon, Stuart was picking up small jobs as well. "My first job was going around the station dumping the wastebasket—especially in the newsroom, where there was always a lot of paper. They paid me spending money." The following summer, he worked as transmitter attendant, a tedious job that involved sitting beside the humming radio equipment in a tiny building out at the antenna site north of the river, taking hourly notes of output levels that seldom varied. Often, when John drove a bag lunch out to Stuart's remote job site, little Catherine would be in the passenger seat, along for the ride. By the time Stuart enrolled at Brandon College (now Brandon University) in a general sciences program in 1951, he was working nights running the master control board. "When the network was on, I'd do my homework. As long as the needle was going back and forth in the console, I knew it was going."

But two years of higher learning persuaded young Stuart that academia was not for him. He enjoyed the social scene and played on the college football and curling squads, but, he admitted, "I wasn't doing that well at all. I was fooling around too much, playing bridge and chasing girls probably." John Craig put no pressure on his son to get into the radio business. But Stuart knew the door was open. "I saw opportunity," he would say later. "I figured, 'I can start right at the bottom and *learn* this business.'" With few regrets, he dropped out of Brandon College and went to work full-time at CKX in 1952.

Johnny Craig's high profile and outgoing style gave everyone in town the impression the station was minting cash. Charismatic and gregarious, Craig was "as close to Hollywood as Brandon got," as grandson Drew would describe him much later. He was also a forward-looking businessman who believed in plowing profits back into his operation and staying abreast of new technology. One of his earliest expenditures, soon after WestMan bought the station, was for an audio recorder; one of the first on the market, it employed steel wire instead of the tape that would be used in future. And when federal regulators at last approved the use of remote controls in place of transmitter attendants (putting an end to the job Stuart found so boring), John Craig acquired Northern Electric's prototype unit for CKX.

But in truth, CKX was no cash cow. Limited by the size of the mainly rural southwestern Manitoba advertising market, Stuart recalled, "The thing never really did make a lot of money. That was [my father's] problem all the way through." What profit did get distributed to shareholders, of course, went mainly to the other investors who held 76 per cent of WestMan's stock. At the end of the day, John Craig never seemed to be in a position to enlarge his stake in the company, even if he had a mind to.

In fact, there seemed little reason to worry about control. No one had any complaints with his management so far. When McDiarmid died in 1952, John Craig easily succeeded him as WestMan's president. And soon the man the staff all called "the Chief" would lead the company—and his investors—into their biggest gamble yet.

Johnny Craig had a wide circle of friends—in sports and business, broadcasting and politics. An active supporter of the Liberals, he'd served a term as provincial party president after the war. He was a founding member of Brandon's Kinsmen's Club, and only the second businessman outside of Winnipeg to be elected president of the Manitoba Chamber of Commerce. An active involvement in the Canadian Association of Broadcasters—as well as travelling to every convention, usually with Catherine at his side, Craig served on the national organization's board in the early 1950s—brought him inside such privileged bastions of the eastern establishment as the Seigneury Club at Montebello in Quebec.

His initial exposure to central Canada left a lasting impression. "The first trip I made left me flabbergasted at the ignorance and lack of interest in western Manitoba on the part of eastern business executives," he told an interviewer in 1955. "It was just like a solid brick wall." It would not be the last time a Craig had reason to lament the limited horizons of Ontario's business and banking class. But over time, John became a respected figure in the national broadcast organization. In turn, he would call it "a privilege to have friendships and contacts with these people. They are smart and broad-minded."

As Craig's network of contacts expanded beyond Manitoba, his trips east became more frequent. He would often join a train at Brandon station only to find one or two fellow broadcasters or Ottawa-bound political players already on board. "A couple of bottles of whiskey later, they'd be in there talking about all these wonderful things that were coming," remembered Stuart, who joined his father on more than a few trips. "They'd tell him he should get into television, it was the wave of the future."

Television's birth was already well in the past. Canadian engineer Reginald Fessenden was one of several researchers who could claim partial paternity of the new medium. But it was another inventive Scot, John Baird, who first showed a fuzzy televised picture to a deeply impressed Royal Academy in London in 1928. Four years later, Baird's equipment was put on display in Ogilvie's Department Store in Montreal, and 100,000 people queued to see silent figures swim across a tiny, red-on-black (sometimes switching unnervingly to black-on-red) screen. In the United States, RCA had been on the point of rolling out a commercial television system in 1940, until Europe's world war refocussed it and other electronic firms on military development instead. Even so, half a dozen American stations made experimental TV broadcasts during the war years, and within twenty-four months of war's end, the promotion of television was in full swing in the United States. By 1949, there were television sets in a million American homes. Two years later, the number was 10 million.

In September 1952, television came to Canada. CBC launched stations in Montreal on September 6 and in Toronto two days later. By then, 146,000 Canadians already owned television sets. Typically, they'd bought them even before there was a single domestic signal to receive. But demand isn't everything in making a market. The Canadian Broadcasting Corporation—in those years both the regulator of the broadcast industry and its largest player—could see that it lacked the capital to build the national transmission system required to supply off-air television to the whole of the country. The buzz in broadcasting circles was that the CBC would open television to private investors, whose stations would become "affiliates" of the public network on the same model as CKX and other stations on its radio network.

By the summer of 1953, John Craig had determined that WestMan should indeed get into television. He'd never seen a set in his life. Undeterred, that October he sent CKX's chief engineer, veteran radio man Humphrey Davies, along with Stuart, to the U.S. National Association of Broadcasters' convention in Chicago. The different manufacturers of transmission systems would all be there, showing off their wares.

The two made the trip by car, stopping at the end of a weary day's drive at Rochester, Minnesota. There they checked into a motel that had a television in each room. The hours on the road forgotten, they switched on the set. "We're starved, we've been driving all day," remembered Stuart, "and we sit in the dark and watch the *Ray Bolger Show*." After tearing themselves reluctantly away from the tube, the intrepid duo grabbed a bite to eat, then tracked down the station's "studios" in a Quonset hut on a hill outside of town. There wasn't much to it: a single camera focussed on a film-chain, a device on which images from up to three film or slide projectors were directed through an array of mirrors to a camera, allowing an operator to switch between the different sources.

In Chicago, three electronics companies had set up giant TV displays in the lobby of the Palmer House Hotel. The one belonging to General Electric featured a working colour camera. That was about as far as the company's technical strength at the convention seemed to run. The salesman who met with the two Canucks, it turned out, had been yanked away from his regular job with G.E. in Winnipeg to work the broadcast convention. He normally sold lightbulbs. He knew nothing at all about television.

But before it could place any orders for a television transmitter, there were a couple of things WestMan needed to nail down: money and a broadcasting licence. There was no way the company could finance the large front-end investment in television out of cash flow. But times were good, and John Craig's business acumen was respected in Brandon. The Bank of Montreal agreed to finance the venture, offering to loan WestMan $250,000—almost four times what Craig and his partners had paid for the company six years earlier.

With that promise in place, Western Manitoba Broadcasters Ltd. applied to the CBC for a television licence. The filing document ran fewer than ten pages, and it was concerned mainly with the technical specs of the proposed service. (By 2000, it would require thousands of pages and up to a million dollars of investment to provide the detailed program proposals, financial statements and public benefit forecasts that the CBC's successor, the CRTC, had come to expect.) If the licence request succeeded, Brandon would become the smallest city in Canada to have its own TV station.

The CBC placed the matter on the agenda for its May 1954 hearings. The hearings were scheduled to be held in St. John's, Newfoundland, at a hotel in the shadow of Signal Hill, the site of Marconi's triumph half a century earlier. John Craig booked a flight to St. John's, and on the day before the hearing Stu drove him to the Winnipeg airport. His plane got as far as Montreal, but the connecting flight was grounded. There was fog in the Newfoundland capital. Fog was still there the next morning—the day of the all-important hearing. John Craig telephoned the hotel where the panel was sitting and pleaded with its chairman not to adjourn without hearing the CKX application. Then he caught a flight that would get into St. John's late in the day—if the fog lifted—after several stops.

Fortunately, by the time the milk run reached the Rock, the air had cleared. Nervous and queasy from the long flight, Craig rushed from the airport to the hearing room, fearing to find it empty. But the chairman had indeed kept the proceedings going, fending off a motion to adjourn to give the representative from CKX the opportunity to submit his application.

Craig's remarks were brief. The new station would be a CBC affiliate, bringing TV to people in southwestern Manitoba currently out of reach of the public service's Winnipeg signal. The Brandon station would be privately financed and (Johnny Craig profoundly hoped) sustained by its own advertising revenue. When he finished speaking, the panellists had only two questions.

"Do you have the money?" one asked. The answer to that was easy.

The only other query came from a panelist with prairie roots. He wanted to know: "How are the Brandon Wheat Kings doing this year, and do you think they'll have a winning team?"

However the Wheat Kings did, Johnny Craig would find out within hours—weeks before it was officially announced—that he had won his TV licence. Heading back west the following day, he happened to run into one of the CBC panellists. "Privately," the fellow indiscreetly confided, "you've got it." John Craig still had not actually seen a television set.

With financing in hand and a permit assured, John set out to raise the bar a little higher. If new studios were needed—as they clearly would be—for television, Craig reasoned that maybe it was also time to say good-bye to the sturdy little red-brick building with the lovely acoustics that had housed CKX Radio for a dozen years. Western Manitoba Broadcasters bought an undeveloped acreage the size of two city blocks on open prairie west of Brandon's built-up limits. Just as the first recession since the war began to close its icy fingers on the prairie economy, the Craigs, father and son, began drawing up blueprints for Canada's first combined radio and television station.

4

Fathers and Sons

The television licence unofficially awarded on John Craig's flight home from Newfoundland did not become a reality until after Labour Day, 1954. Within days of receiving the CBC's official confirmation, Craig turned the sod for a new broadcast complex, shrugging off a persistent autumn drizzle that chilled the small group of directors who stood beside him as the bright blade dug into prairie loam. With characteristic eagerness to get at the job—and a habitual eye to the promotional potential—Craig set December 24 as the target date for the station's launch. Television would be CKX's Christmas present to Brandon.

The next three months were a frenzy of activity. The new studio site was beyond city services and had to be connected (at WestMan's cost) to Brandon water and sewer lines. A building was needed, with separate spaces for radio and television studios, newsroom and record library, and common offices for TV and radio sales staff. Radio engineers, operators and announcers, many of whom expected to transfer to television or do duty on both sides of the expanded operation, needed to learn new skills and the mechanics of new equipment. Canadian General Electric undertook to deliver a transmitter in time for the planned holiday sign-on; it would have to be wired in, tuned and tested. Construction began on a 76-metre tower to hold a vertical array of four bat-wing television antennas that would add another 15 metres to its height.

But the Christmas present was not to be. As the first of December came and went, the building stood, but other installations lagged. It was not until mid-January that all the critical components of the new transmitter were connected, tested and brought up to power. Compared with the computer-laden command bridge of a modern television studio, the state-of-the-art suite of 1955 was a crude affair. It consisted of one camera, one film-chain, one control board (essentially for switching between the camera and the film-chain) and a 19,500-watt television

Left: John B. Craig and Catherine (Middleton) Craig married on September 1, 1928, and soon moved into a small brick-and-stucco bungalow on 22nd Street in Brandon, their home for the next four decades.

Right: Craig Motors Ltd. opened its doors at the corner of Louise Avenue and 10th Street a year before the stock market collapse of 1929 unleashed the Great Depression. (The site is now occupied by the new Brandon City Hall.)

Left: To meet demand for daily farm market reports, the Manitoba Telephone Service erected towers beside Brandon's original City Hall (since demolished) and began broadcasting. During World War II, the original frame studio was replaced by a sturdy little red-brick building (*facing page*).

Left: By the late 1930s, CKX's daily programming had expanded from a few hours to dawn-to-midnight news and entertainment. Live musical programs featuring local performers were popular. A few years later, during World War II, listeners throughout south-western Manitoba would tune to CKX Radio each evening for news from the battlefront. Reports were frequently laced with the sound of live gunfire.

CKX
BROADCAST
- BOOTH -

As part of the Canadian Broadcasting Corporation's "Dominion" network in the days before audiotape, CKX relied on extra-long-play "transcription" records made of shellac, which contained entire radio programs.

Left: When John Craig led a group of Brandon investors to buy CKX from the Manitoba Telephone Service in 1948, the station had 23 employees. Craig cut the number to 18—and doubled the sales team, to 2. He named the new company Western Manitoba Broadcasters Ltd.

Facing page: Johnny Craig *(left)* had been a star goalie for the Brandon Wheat Kings. In 1938, while working as advertising sales manager for CKX, he pioneered the concept of live, play-by-play hockey broadcasting.

Above: CKX's new studio building on Victoria Avenue, opened in 1954, was the first in Canada built to house both radio and television broadcasting studios.

Above: Engineers operate the control panel for CKX Television. On the first night of broadcasting, families lined sidewalks outside store windows in downtown Brandon, where televisions were set up to display the new technology.

Facing page: "Bat-wing" transmission antennas are shown arriving at the studio construction site. Once lifted 90 metres into the air, the antennas radiated a 19,500-volt signal—a fraction the power of today's CKX.

Above: The station's first television camera was black-and-white only, had no zoom lens, and weighed so much that it travelled on its own permanent dolly.

Above: The station's first cameraman was Stuart Craig, who is shown here operating the camera for CKX's first entertainment series, the *Roy Brown Variety Show.* With only one camera and no means of recording video, "you had to be creative," Stu remembered later.

Right: Manitoba Premier Douglas Campbell congratulates John B. Craig at the official opening of CKX Television in September 1955. The opening was delayed for six months by Craig's near-fatal heart attack that spring. Shown *left to right* are: Brandon mayor Jim Creighton, Catherine Craig, John Craig, Campbell and Wilf Carpenter from CBC Winnipeg.

transmitter tuned to VHF Channel 5. No special-effects generator, no banks of videotape recorders, no satellite down-link monitors: those technologies did not yet exist. And it would be months before the space designated for CKX Radio operations was ready for occupancy. But CKX Television was ready to roll—and neither Craig was willing to wait a moment longer to try it out.

On January 17, 1955, everything was turned on and the transmitter brought up to full power. From the bat-wings 91 metres overhead, CKX Television beamed out the first picture ever to travel through the electromagnetic air space of southwestern Manitoba: a test-pattern slide of target circles and a single, incongruous Indian chief's head in full feathered headdress. People watched it. They not only watched, they phoned the Brandon *Sun* to report how well the signal came in.

Eleven days later, at 7:00 p.m. on January 28, the real thing came to Brandon. The new station's broadcast life began with a short statement from Johnny Craig, followed by a half-hour news- and sportscast—all done the only way it could be: live-to-air. The *Liberace Show* (on film) came next, then a movie wrapped up the four-hour programming block. During live portions of the inaugural broadcast, Stuart ran the station's single camera. Afterward, John and Catherine Craig invited the station staff back to the two-bedroom bungalow on 22nd Street for a party to celebrate their accomplishment.

There were, perhaps, 100 television sets within reach of CKX's signal.

But there was no mistaking the public's eagerness for the new medium. In downtown Brandon, several Rosser Street merchants with televisions in stock placed them in their store windows and tuned them to Channel 5. Hundreds of men and women, even entire families, braved the cold, wet night to stand outside and witness the new electronic genie being born. And when, months later, Manitoba Premier Douglas Campbell attended the official opening of the combined radio-television complex, the Brandon *Sun* (like many newspapers over the years, not always a supporter of broadcast rivals for local advertising), put the news in three-inch headline type across the front of a two-part supplement: "TELEVISION IS HERE." The paper was full of display ads for televisions made by G.E., RCA, Sylvania, Westinghouse and Crosley.

That official ribbon-cutting would be put off until September, however. On May 17, before he could move into his own new office—the last area of the new station scheduled to be finished—the ebullient, fifty-seven-year-old John Craig was struck down by a heart attack. The attack was happily not fatal, but in keeping with medical practice of the day, Craig's doctors ordered an extended convalescence in the confines of the Brandon Hospital. For months, the newborn television station would manage without its founding spirit.

In his father's place, twenty-one-year-old Stuart Craig found himself thrown into the role of acting chief executive, making critical decisions about what programs the station would buy for broadcast in its first full season ahead. In truth, Stuart reflected later, "I knew about as much about the TV business as he did, because he had no experience either."

Although John Craig would return to work in time to shake Premier Campbell's hand at the ribbon-cutting, he would never again exhibit the same boundless energy he once had. In the years ahead, he would increasingly draw back from day-to-day involvement in WestMan's management; Stuart's role would steadily expand.

By the time of its delayed formal opening, CKX Television was broadcasting daily from 5:00 to 11:00 p.m.—with an hour off between 6:00 and 7:00 for "televiewers," as they were called, to eat dinner with the family before settling in for an evening of television. In addition to the kitschy but popular *Liberace Show,* the station's line-up included *Dragnet,* the *Art Linkletter Show,* the transplanted radio staple *Amos 'n' Andy* and the Ray Bolger variety show that had transfixed Stu the first time he saw a television. As its staff gained confidence in the new medium, CKX began adding productions of its own. The first to go to air was the *Roy Brown Variety Show,* a half-hour local talent showcase. The *Ranch House* show, a country and western program, would soon follow.

It took considerable planning to choreograph a newscast—let alone a live half-hour variety show—to go to air seamlessly. "We had only one camera, no zoom lenses," remembered Stuart. "You had to use your imagination." Whenever the camera pulled away from one shot, under cover of a slide from the film-chain, the next shot had to be set up and ready immediately, or audiences would be stuck watching the slide until it was. And if a performer lost his or her place in mid-sentence, well, they just *did* ... and everyone watching television in Brandon knew about it.

The rudimentary technology imparted a spontaneous quality to sponsorship messages missing from commercials today. On one occasion, a camera-store owner, in mounting panic, managed to shred the photograph being printed by the new Polaroid camera he was attempting to demonstrate. On another, a novelty-store proprietor brought a trick coin-box to show off during his live ad. It was equipped with an alarm that triggered the moment he opened the device on camera and refused to go off throughout the rest of his distracted sales pitch. "We were in the control room, killing ourselves," Stuart admitted, looking back. "That was a fun time."

But if live television had pitfalls, early programming from the CBC network had its own shortcomings. The capacity to transmit television signals live across the country would not come until CKX had been on the air for more than two years. Until that time, a technique called kinescope was used to distribute network programming. "The quality," Stuart recalled, "was just brutal." Network shows were filmed by a camera focussed on a television monitor at the studio where the production originated; copies of the film then went to network affiliates by mail. The results were often grainy and dark (wrestling shows, produced in underlit arenas, were the worst) and always late. The Christmas edition of the *Ed Sullivan Show* arrived in Brandon in the second week of January.

Stuart Craig would never have any doubts about the wisdom of his decision to enter broadcasting. But within six months of helping put CKX Television on the air, his life would change irrevocably on another front. Looking back over his career more than forty-five years later, he would still call it the most important event of his life. The moment, he said, was "when I started going out with my wife."

Stuart had, in fact, gone out with Shirley Finch's younger sister, Betty, first. The Finches were the "girls next door," growing up just across 22nd Street from the Craig family. Their father, Percy, was an insurance agent. By 1955 both Finch daughters were working as clerks at the Great West Coal Co.—jobs that put them in the enviable position of having the summer months almost entirely off. Slender and pretty, with light-brown hair and blue eyes, Shirley for a while double-dated with Betty and Stuart and one of Stuart's pals. But sometime that spring, Stuart remembers, "All of a sudden, it just happened." By fall the two were going steady. And on June 2, 1956—Stuart's twenty-third birthday—they married in St. Paul's United Church. With only a little regret, the newlywed husband sold his treasured metallic blue Dodge to put a down payment on a tidy bungalow half a dozen blocks from the street where both their parents lived.

It was the beginning of what, by every measure, would be the most important relationship in Stuart Craig's life. "She was my partner," Stuart said simply. "We shared everything." Without overpowering career ambitions of her own, Shirley fell easily and, by all accounts contentedly, into the role of housewife and later house-mother to a growing family of rambunctious young Craig males. "She always made sure we had at least one good meal a day," Stuart said. More importantly, "She was a very honest, honest person." Unflappable and unstintingly kind, Shirley took the lead in creating a home environment that fostered family loyalty, self-confidence and an affectionate tolerance for others' quirks—in a word, love.

The couple's partnership went beyond domestic things. Shirley had keen business judgement, which Stuart respected deeply. He held nothing about the business back from her. "She saw the financial statements. She knew everything that was going on at the station. Every time a decision came along, she was always part of it."

For their honeymoon, the couple had planned to tour the northwestern United States on the way to a convention of the Western Association of Broadcasters at Banff Springs. The plan broke down along with the CKX Ford in Havre, Montana. Rental cars were rarer then and unavailable in Havre. And, in any case, Stu and Shirley didn't have the money to rent a car. The newlyweds made do with the romantic possibilities of a small roadside motel and a "pretty good" local diner for four or five days, waiting for Ford to send parts to fix the car. They did make it to the convention—but the tour of the Northwest had to be scrapped.

By the summer of 1956, more than a year after it went on air, television was at last beginning to contribute positively to Western Manitoba Broadcasters' bottom line. The Next Big Thing had not automatically turned into a money machine. CKX might have spent a bundle to launch Brandon into the TV age, but the Brandon advertising market wasn't a whole lot bigger than it had been before Liberace came to town. Advertisers still had other outlets for their messages, including the newspaper and the Craigs's own CKX Radio, both of which reached far more Brandon consumers than owned television sets. (It's possible, too, that some potential advertisers, after witnessing their competitors' star-crossed live commercials, decided their own interests might be better served by staying as far away as possible from this dangerous new medium.) On the other hand, anyone who did buy time on television was assured of a 100 per cent market share—a grail that exists today only in broadcasters' dreams. There was, quite simply, nothing else on.

And if Western Manitoba's revenues were climbing, so were costs. In addition to the drag on cash flow of retiring the debt taken on to expand into television, the initial investment in the new technology would plainly not be the last if CKX were to keep pace with the medium's rapid evolution. Fuelling that development was a new field of Cold War rivalry: space. The Soviet Union's launch of the first man-made satellite, *Sputnik,* in 1957, launched the superpowers into a race for extraterrestrial dominance that would, twelve years later, put men on the moon. Meanwhile, the exploration of space energized a quantum leap in communications technology. The new Brandon facility, considered ground-breaking when it was built—broadcasters from across the country sent teams of engineers to examine how CKX had combined television and radio stations—would nonetheless soon needed upgrading.

In the same year that *Sputnik* went up, the CBC inaugurated a 6,300-kilometre cross-Canada microwave network—the longest in the world—and CKX installed the necessary receiving equipment to be a charter member. The national network put an end to bleached-out kinescope copies of *Ed Sullivan* and, for the first time, allowed the national public broadcaster to reach all of Canada's largest centres at once. In Brandon, CKX Television operators mastered the precision task of timing a local program to meet the network schedule with neither overlap nor an embarrassing silence.

The Craigs were looking further ahead. Seizing on the potential of microwaves, CKX ordered an additional system in early 1958, and that summer put it to what, at the time, was radical use. The Manitoba Exhibition, held each year on grounds just south of Brandon, was the centrepiece of the entire region's summer calendar. Ever the showman, Johnny Craig had CKX engineers install a microwave transmitter on a rooftop at the fairgrounds, the antenna aimed back at CKX's tower on the western edge of the city. Carpenters built a temporary studio stage in one of the exhibition halls. With its inaugural broadcast from the fair, CKX pioneered the live TV remote much as it had the live radio remote thirty years earlier. Then, it had been Craig Sr. who called the plays of a hockey game. Now, Craig Jr. manned the sole CKX camera as it panned over entertainers who sang, danced and told jokes during half-hourly cut-ins on regular programming. Fairgoers by the hundreds pressed forward for a better look at the mysteries of television-in-the-making. The CKX remote (later moved to a permanent pavilion on the fairgrounds) would continue to be one of the most popular attractions at the exhibition for another decade.

But the summer of 1958 would stand out for Stuart and Shirley Craig for other reasons. On August 31, Shirley delivered a healthy baby boy. He was christened John Andrew Craig, but from the start would go by Drew (sometimes, among family, "Drooper," after a comedy character on TV). In his spare time, Stuart renovated the modest 28th Street bungalow to accommodate a growing family.

At work as well, Stuart was taking on new responsibilities. Never the natural extrovert his father was, Stu displayed a reserve in the office that, over the years, would turn into a shell of brusqueness. It concealed a sensitive side that he shared with Shirley and the family, as well as a slapstick sense of humour that only occasionally came out on the job. (Although he did participate in his share of the practical jokes that are—or used to be—an integral part of broadcasting culture. On one occasion, Stu secretly tapped into another staff member's home TV antenna and succeeded in inserting a phony commercial—delivered only to the victim's house—seamlessly into the regular station programming. The follicly challenged fellow got to watch himself as the unwitting before-and-after model for a line of toupées. "The next day we went around telling everyone how good he looked on TV," Craig chortled as he recounted the story. "He thought it was really on the air.")

But anything Stuart may have lacked in the way of his father's inborn salesman's charm, he more than made up for with his appetite for hard work. "Mr. Craig Senior was a very firm man," says retired station engineer Lawrence Dubois. "A very fair man but a very firm man. I think he was harder on [Stuart] than he was on the rest of us." In the Craig universe, family would never be an excuse for failing to do your job.

By late 1958, television was generating enough income to justify the acquisition of a second camera. The following year, the transmitter received more power, and the television studio space was enlarged.

Radio was changing too. With the advent of TV, radio's "Golden Age," as many would later recall it, began its long fade-out. By the end of the fifties, network radio shows in the form of distinct, scheduled program segments—variety, mystery and comedy programming—had all but disappeared. Most of the broadcast day was filled with the breezy blend of popular music and disc-jockey patter that would dominate commercial radio for the rest of the century. One-person announcer/operators had done away with the need to hire two people to perform those functions separately. The changes reduced staff needs significantly. It proved fortunate for some CKX employees that radio's transformation had coincided with WestMan's venture into television.

As the fifties closed and a new decade began, Stuart and Shirley Craig had double reason to celebrate. On Valentine's Day, 1960, their family expanded once more when Drew gained a baby brother, Thomas Boyd (like his older sibling and their father, he would go by his second name). Then, in August of that year, Stuart's expanding role at the station was recognized when he joined the Western Manitoba Broadcasters' board of directors. He was three months past his twenty-seventh birthday.

After the stability of the 1950s, the new decade brought unprecedented social turbulence to North America. The economy boomed like never before or since: 1960 was the first of more than twenty unbroken years of economic expansion in Canada (although inflation would badly erode the boom's benefits after 1970). The turmoil was elsewhere, on the cultural and political fronts.

In Ottawa, Conservative Prime Minister John Diefenbaker, a prairie visionary whose thundering oratory owed much to his years as a courtroom lawyer, surrendered office to a succession of minority Liberal governments led by a lisping, low-key diplomat, Lester Pearson. Canadians would not entrust a leader with a majority mandate again until 1968, when they swept a charismatic forty-eight-year-old Quebecker with intellectual combat skills honed by the Jesuits into office, on a wave of Trudeaumania. For a brief season at the end of the decade, Ottawa would feel almost like a northern Camelot.

By then, the United States' flirtation with its Camelot had come and gone, ending in national tragedy. For many Americans, Democratic President John F. Kennedy's assassination in November 1963 would come to be regarded as the initial act of a progressive madness that would engulf their country in an epidemic of gratuitous violence. It was also the first event for which television, which followed the murder and its aftermath to the exclusion of all else, provided the medium for the shared horror, grief and memory of an entire continent.

Before his untimely death, Kennedy had committed the United States to an unwinnable war in Vietnam which his successor, Lyndon Johnson, found politically unsaleable as well. Divided public views on the conflict turned many of America's own cities into fields of battle and overshadowed Johnson's considerable success at breaking down the barriers of race. In the same year that Canadians gave Liberal Pierre Trudeau a majority government, Americans elected a conservative Republican, Richard Nixon, as president. By the end of the sixties, Nixon's brooding presence in the White House would polarize American society still further between self-styled conservative "patriots" and the so-called liberal "counterculture" of anti-war protesters, civil rights demonstrators and Magic Bus hippies.

It would all be played out for Canadians on TV—alongside the Beatles, *I Spy,* spaghetti westerns, *Reach for the Top* (with its dapper host Alex Trebek), and the serial extravaganzas of Canada's centennial year in 1967. Brandon, like most Canadian towns and smaller cities, would remain essentially untouched by the political passions burning elsewhere.

For Johnny Craig's grandchildren, "it was a great place to grow up," recalls the eldest, Drew. "There were really no 'rich kids' and 'poor kids.'" Instead, there were pick-up games of street hockey on the looping oxbow of Cedar Bay Crescent, where Stuart and Shirley bought a pie-shaped lot within sight of the CKX studios in 1961. The property was hardly palatial, just a comfortably middle-class suburban home. But it had a big back yard and a modern split-level, with enough room for an expected third addition to the family. The arrival of Stuart Miles that September—he would never use the "Stuart," but after metrification would sometimes answer to "Kilo"—would round out Shirley's hat trick of sons.

But if prosperous stability endured into the sixties for longer in southwestern Manitoba than in some other places, the next few years would nonetheless bring tribulations to the Craig family from unexpected quarters.

The most dramatic of these occurred on a spring day in the year of Miles's birth. Once again, the station was upgrading: this time, with a new antenna and tower that would quadruple CKX-TV's signal strength to 100,000 watts. The new tower was to replace the existing one, behind the Brandon studio building. Erecting it was a delicate task, as contractors extended each slender section of tower upwards with the aid of a moveable, 46-metre splint called a "gin pole," which held the new section in place until it could be secured. This was done by workers aloft and below, who attached the new part to the previously raised tower and strung guy wires in three directions to the ground. As the tower neared its planned 162-metre height, the guy wires rising from earth to the top of the soaring stick became progressively steeper. The rising angle of the wires also made them increasingly unstable, the same way a ladder with its foot too near the house becomes unstable. It was a risk factor the contractor chose to disregard.

On the morning of May 27, all was set to erect the last and highest section of all: the 25-metre antenna mast, which would sit atop the tower cap, already 137 metres above the prairie. In preparation, the gin pole was raised higher still, less than half of it now overlapping the guyed tower. At about eleven o'clock that morning, tragedy struck.

An inquest would later determine it was a matter of physics and the contractor's oversight. Somehow, the centre of gravity of the gin pole had been allowed to rise above the point at which it remained attached to the tower. Suddenly top-heavy, the massive pole fell away from the vertical, flipping end-to-end on the few steel bolts holding its foot to the tower. For terrifying seconds the gin pole hung there, swinging like a giant pendulum from the top of the tower as the shriek of overstressed steel ripped through the morning air. Clinging to the tower cap, where they had been stationed ready to secure the antenna mast, workmen Auriel Filion and Gilles Côté could only watch and pray. Then the wildly swinging gin pole tore away two of the three sets of guy wires holding the whole tower aloft. In seconds, the huge stick collapsed to the ground in a tangle of bent steel and twisted cable. Filion and Côté were dead.

Liability for the accident lay with the contractor. The financial blow to CKX was contained by insurance. Even so, the two deaths left the entire station staff shaken—as did the hideous thought of what might have happened if the tower had fallen in any direction other than the one it had. "That was the worst day of my career, I'll tell you that," Stuart remembered sadly. (Much later, Miles would use exactly the same words to describe the day in 1997 when David Yachison, a senior technician with the family company's wireless cable system, was killed in an electrical accident.) The power increase for CKX-TV would come soon enough, when a second tower was raised, without incident, on an open field three kilometres from the station. But from then on, unwritten company policy would require every tower WestMan built to be located far enough away from other structures to ensure that none could be harmed in a collapse. Subsequently, new safety standards also reduced the likelihood of another gin pole becoming top-heavy.

And there would be many more towers over the years. Cost-effective microwave transmission had also made possible remote rebroadcasting units. In effect, these were unattended little television stations, fed with programming from a home studio via microwave, that could serve an audience too small to sustain a full station of its own. After securing approvals from the Board of Broadcast Governors (which had taken over the licensing of private broadcasters from the CBC in 1958), CKX added "rebroads" in Melita and Foxwarren, communities 100 kilometres southwest and northwest of Brandon. The investments substantially expanded the station's potential audience.

But it was yet another event of 1961, one that seemed remote and almost inconsequential compared to the new bundle of joy in the Craig home or the fatal tower collapse, that would bring a corrosive element into the family's erstwhile warm relationship with the community it both served and depended upon. On New Year's Day that year, CFTO-TV, owned by Toronto *Telegram* publisher John Bassett, went on the air in the Ontario capital. Toronto was the first city in Canada to have two television stations. Bassett's station was one of eight "second-service" licences the Board of Broadcast Governors had approved the previous year. By the end of 1961, new private stations were also operating in Montreal, Ottawa, Vancouver, Calgary, Edmonton and Halifax—and in Winnipeg, where the Moffat family, having missed the first wave of television, launched a station with the call sign CJAY.

The following year, CJAY applied to put a rebroadcaster in Brandon.

The Craigs were shaken. Their own stations were paying their bills and spinning off enough profit to keep abreast of new techology—radio added an FM service in 1963; television acquired a tape video recorder in 1965 and began to add colour in 1966—but that was about it. A second network signal would fragment the small Brandon television audience (28,000 people in 1961). Worse, a new station was bound to be followed by CJAY salesmen eager to cut a slice from CKX's local advertising revenue. Western Manitoba Broadcasters intervened against the CJAY application, arguing that the local market could not sustain the additional service.

The Board of Broadcast Governors agreed, and they turned CJAY down. The Moffat-owned station would try repeatedly over the years that followed to bring its signal to Brandon. As often, CKX would present the case that the market was too thin to support it. Each time, the regulators would agree that the Craigs' fears were well founded. As a result, it would be a decade before second service came to Brandon. But viewers wanted the extra programming, and the delay in getting it would deeply strain the community's relations with the Craigs. The animosity only deepened after Bassett organized several of the independent stations into a cooperative national network called CTV in 1965. Relations chilled still more when the new network stole the contract to televise Canadian Football League games—including those of the Winnipeg Blue Bombers—away from the CBC. Deprived of weekend football on the tube, angry Brandonites blamed the Craigs.

In practice, that meant they blamed Stuart. After a second heart attack in 1963, Johnny Craig, then sixty-two, effectively retired from management of the radio and television stations, although he and Catherine would continue attending national and regional broadcasting conventions, as much for their social as their business value, until her death. In 1968, Stuart was named managing director. The following year, at age thirty-five, he replaced John Craig as president of Western Manitoba Broadcasters. Craig Sr. still cut a colourful if portly figure, tooling around town in his coral-tone Cadillac. But his larger-than-life personal style served only to persuade many in Brandon that the Craigs and "their" station must be rolling in cash. "There was a lot of jealousy in the community," is how Stu put it years later. "They thought we were making a bundle of money, that I was handed the station." A fallacy on both counts.

"It was a tough time for me and my wife," Stuart remembered. "People were against us in the community. They thought we were keeping CTV out—and they were right. But we had to protect our business interests."

The defence took an increasing emotional toll. The Brandon *Sun*, perhaps understandably, championed the cause of CTV-hungry viewers. Possibly inadvertently, it also helped stir up resentment against the Craigs. Local politicians demonstrated in front of the station. Stu and

Shirley almost stopped going out. Drew and Boyd, both by now in school, felt the pressure in playground taunts and even some sharp-edged comments from teachers. "It didn't bother me," Drew says now. "We didn't get the brunt of it. But it was damaging and hurtful to my mom and dad."

Brandon was not the only smaller centre where local broadcasters felt threatened by public pressure for a second television service. Soon federal regulators moved to ease the tensions. In 1967, they ruled that small-market TV broadcasters could own two station licences, one affiliated with the CBC, the other with CTV, and mount both transmitters on a single tower—an approach that came to be known as a "twin stick" operation. Stuart Craig was the first broadcaster to apply under the new policy to "twin stick" a CTV service alongside CKX's existing CBC programming. He was turned down.

Stuart went back to the drawing board.

Soon a new threat rocked the family. It could be dated from October 1969. That month, John and Catherine Craig attended a broadcast convention in Vancouver. Catherine, who had injured her foot just before the trip, wore carpet slippers everywhere in the damp autumn weather and returned to Brandon with a cold. Within days, she was dead. Stuart, who had always been close to his mother (closer even, his sister believes, than he had been to their father), was deeply shaken.

Stuart was rattled in a different way the following spring. A member of WestMan's board of directors phoned him with the tip that someone was trying to seize control of the company Stuart had spent almost half his life building.

It had never, of course, been "his" company in a legal sense. Stuart Craig owned only 30 of Western Manitoba Broadcasters' 5,900 common shares, acquired in small parcels over the years. True, John Craig owned another 2,100. But that was still short of the 2,951 shares that would give the Craigs control. And as Stuart soon discovered, "Dad had only two [other] shareholders he could count on—for 51 per cent, total."

Some shareholders might well have regarded their investment in the company as less than sterling. CKX Radio and Television were supporting their staff and management—on a modest scale—and generating enough cash flow to stay on top of technical developments in the industry. But, as Stuart freely admitted in retrospect, "We could never get the revenue up high enough so the shareholders got paid." So when Winnipeg accountant and minority WestMan investor Edson Boyd, backed by board member Jack Elviss and David Lang, the local Brandon bottler of Coca-Cola, began gathering up smaller stakes in early 1970, their chances of toppling the Craig management seemed more than reasonable.

Word of the takeover plot exploded the domestic calm at 35 Cedar Bay Crescent as effectively as a mortar landing in the back garden. "I'd be about ten years old," recalls Drew. "My mom and dad were practically in tears. It looked like we might lose the station, like we might have to move out of Brandon entirely. It was a very tough time."

But if the conspirators thought the younger Craig lacked the juice to hold on to the company his father had founded, they were dead wrong. Stuart, supported by John, arranged a credit line from the Bank of Montreal and began approaching other minority shareholders. That October, he was able to pick up two significant stock blocks, totalling 655 shares. It was progress, and it seemed to break the other side's momentum. It still wasn't control.

The key to that seemed to reside with 300 shares that Elviss and Boyd held in WestMan through Manalta Investment Company Ltd., registered in Winnipeg. But Elviss and Boyd's position in Manalta was vulnerable. For some years, mercurial Winnipeg broadcaster Jack Oscar Blick (who had given his initials to radio station CJOB in the city) had represented Manalta to federal regulators as a company under his control. Elviss and Boyd had gone along with the subterfuge. When their role in Manalta came to light in correspondence reaching the Craigs, and with their takeover attempt running out of steam, Boyd and Elviss folded. After concluding transactions with Boyd on Christmas Eve, 1971, and with Elviss the following month, Stuart wound up with Manalta Investments—and with 300 more shares. The shares finally gave the Craigs, *pere* and *fils*, bulletproof control of CKX. Manalta, which Stuart maintained, would eventually become the holding company for his position in Western Manitoba Broadcasters—later Craig Broadcast Systems Inc.

Stuart would keep assembling shares—sometimes impetuously—in what could at last properly be called *his* company, for years. (The last handful, in fact, would not come into his hands until July 1999.) He would also keep struggling to bring some vigour to the company's anaemic bottom line.

The two issues came together at WestMan's annual meeting in 1972.

One substantial minority shareholder, a judge named John Kerr, attended the evening affair for the first time. He was incensed at what he denounced as the Craigs' wasteful management. "He claimed [we] were taking huge salaries out of the company and not paying enough dividends," Stuart remembered. "After about five minutes of him calling my dad and me every name under the sun, I got mad. I showed him our salaries right out of the paybook." The judge had to concede their reasonableness, but still insisted he wanted to sell his 800 shares in WestMan. "I said I'd buy them."

The judge instructed Craig to be in his chambers the next morning at nine. At the appointed time, Stuart appeared and, in his neat hand, wrote out two cheques for a total of $104,375. The judge turned over the stock certificates. The two shook hands and Stuart left, in mounting apprehension. He had nothing close to $104,375 in his bank account. And he had not had time to warn his banker he was going to be making such a heavy call on his line of credit.

Outside the courthouse, he turned toward the bank and picked up his pace. "I'm going down one side of 10th Street," Stu recounted, "and I look over and the judge is going down the other side of the street, and he's just *giving* it." Craig redoubled his efforts, reaching his bank moments before the judge got to his. Walking straight in on the manager, Stu breathlessly warned him that his telephone was about to ring—and why.

Gulping, the manager advised his client, "I can't authorize a loan that size without approval from Winnipeg and Toronto."

"The matter's done," Craig told him. "That phone is going to ring."

As if on cue, it did. Stuart held his breath as the bankers exchanged brief pleasantries. He heard his man tell the caller, "Those cheques are as good as gold," and felt himself relax. Then the banker threw Stu out: he had some calls of his own to make!

But the fight for control was not quite over. After his wife's death, Johnny Craig, ever the *bon vivant,* had caught the eye of a striking woman twelve years his junior, a vivacious and successful Brandon travel agent named Doreen Rungay. In short order, Rungay had separated from her husband and was keeping company with Johnny B.

As the second-time-around romance grew hotter and ever more likely to end at the altar, John's son began to feel fresh alarm for his hold on WestMan. Stuart was already close to $90,000 in debt from share purchases so far, but more than two-thirds of the stock that represented Craig family control of the company remained in his father's hands. On the other hand, Craig Sr.'s stock represented the core of the elder Craig's financial security. After some discussion, the two men reached an agreement acceptable to both. Stuart would buy his father's stock over time, at the same price he had paid for other blocks. John would continue to sit on WestMan's board and receive director's fees. There was only one other condition: Stuart must *not* tell Doreen of the deal. He agreed.

When the agreement eventually did come to light, it would add an extra twist to one of the most gut-wrenching tests of Stuart Craig's life.

5

Roots of Rivalry

Nineteen seventy-two had begun well. It would only get better. Much as they missed Catherine, the younger Craigs could at least take satisfaction that their widowed father was not leading a hermit's life. John and Doreen Craig had a busy social calendar in Brandon. In winter, they travelled to Mexico, and in the summer once to Scotland, where John revisited the home he had last laid eyes upon as a seven-year-old boy.

Meanwhile, the relief of settling the control issue was followed by a welcome and long-sought resolution to the deadlock over CTV's entry into Brandon. Negotiations with the other players in Manitoba television—CBC, CTV and the private network's Winnipeg affiliate owned by the Moffat family—had started, stalled, broken down and started again several times over the years. Finally, Stuart and the Moffats had reached an agreement that seemed to work for everyone. And on December 20, 1972, Stu finally got to make Brandonites the Christmas present of a television station: CKY-B Brandon. Broadcasting from a newly built, 412-metre tower south of the city, the station was owned by a newly incorporated entity called Relay Communications. Relay Communications, in turn, was owned in equal 50 per cent shares by WestMan and Moffat Communications.

In fact, CKY-B was essentially a rebroadcaster for Moffat's home station in Winnipeg—which had acquired its new call letters in the 1960s—with one small but critical difference. The programming was identical—right down to the ardently desired CFL games. But whenever the Moffat station broadcast a Winnipeg retailer's television commercial, CKX had the right to cut that ad out of the signal and substitute a commercial for a Brandon retailer instead, while keeping the revenue from the Brandon sale. In addition, a formula gave WestMan a slice of CKY's national revenue, representing the Brandon audience's share of CKY's total viewership. "Every time they sold a commercial,

I got a piece of the action—plus I got all the local ads," Stuart Craig would long and wistfully remember. "It was a beautiful deal for us." It would endure for fourteen years.

But CTV's entry into the market would hurt WestMan's revenue in other respects. National ad sales fell off dramatically when many Canada-wide sponsors realized they could add the Brandon audience to their "buy" more cheaply by advertising on CKY (thus getting viewers in Winnipeg *and* Brandon) than by making a stand-alone buy on CKX. Even so, WestMan's overall earnings began to increase. In the first twenty-four years of its existence, until 1972, operating profits had climbed into six figures only three times (and dipped as low as $58,100 in 1970, the year that sparked Boyd and Elviss's shareholder revolt). With Relay contributing to earnings, and even taking into account the drop-off in national revenues to CKX, Western Manitoba's profits would climb steadily for most of the decade ahead, dropping only when recession and soaring interest rates put their teeth into the economy in 1980. Stuart, meanwhile, exercised his hard-won voting control to put an end to the cash drain of paying regular dividends: for the next two decades, WestMan operating profits would go back into the business.

If CKX's finances were on a more stable footing, the Craig family accounts were still strained. Altogether, Stuart had borrowed nearly $275,000 to finance his various share purchases. Now he and Shirley pinched pennies to pay the debt off as quickly as possible. Despite their well-heeled image in Brandon, recalls second son Boyd, "I had friends who always seemed to have more money than I did."

Family friend Bob Cornell, a Brandon plumbing and heating contractor who would later become a partner with Stuart in several land-development ventures, similarly remembers that the Craigs "struggled in those days."

At the limit of his credit, Stuart was forced to pass on an opportunity he would always regret. H. Gordon Love, who had started a CTV affiliate, CFCN-TV, in Calgary in the mid-sixties, had died. Love's family—with one exception—now wanted to cash out of the business. They made Craig an offer that would have left CKX in the hands of the one Love son who wanted to stay in broadcasting, while Craig got CFCN for something in the neighbourhood of $3 million. "I could trade up," he remembered. "But I'd just bought the shares in the company. I had no money, and I couldn't get any money." As always, the problem was revenue: Brandon and southwestern Manitoba simply had too few people to attract rich advertising campaigns. If the Craig broadcasting enterprise was to match its potential, it would have to find new audiences.

In 1973, the CRTC seemed to hold out the hope of just that. Twenty-one years after television's arrival in Manitoba, and eleven years after "second service" had made its appearance, the federal broadcast regulator had decided that Manitoba's capital was ready for a third local television service. WestMan, in Stuart's view, was the obvious candidate for the new licence. CKX had proven its capabilities many times over in the two decades since it pioneered television in the province's southwest. Surely the CRTC would agree it had the depth of experience to deliver the desired "third service" to Winnipeg. Certainly, a Winnipeg licence would cure WestMan's small-market revenue blues.

Once again, Stuart visited his bankers. After getting their blessing, he began assembling an application—a far more complex proposition now than it had been when Johnny Craig had secured CKX-TV's first permit on the basis of a ten-page document.

Then, WestMan had been the only company willing to take a plunge into the risky, capital-intensive television business. Now that the medium was a proven money-spinner, however, the latest CRTC call attracted interest from several quarters. And this time, Stuart Craig would run up against an adversary whose operating principles were very different from his own, a wily and persuasive backroom player unafraid of wielding an influence that ran wide and deep—especially within the Liberal Party that held the reins of power in Ottawa.

Stuart Craig and Israel Harold Asper—known as "Izzy" to everyone—were born only forty kilometres and ten months apart. Asper, the elder of the two, was the child of a movie-house owner in Minnedosa, a one-street farming town tucked into the verdant valley of the Saskatchewan River north of Brandon. In the happy years of the early fifties, Asper, Stuart Craig and Shirley Finch had been part of the same young social crowd that flowed to and from events in Brandon, Minnedosa and other smaller centres in the region. Asper had even once carried Shirley's roller skates back to her home on 22nd Street from an outing at the local roller rink.

Exceptionally bright and ambitious, Asper moved to Winnipeg after high school and secured a law degree in 1957. Over the next decade, he became a leading tax expert, sharing his advice with a national audience as a financial columnist. He also forged the first of several friendships that would prove strategic when his law firm accepted a young articling student named Gerald Schwartz as an employee. (Much later, Schwartz would make a bid to buy up and unite Canada's two national airlines.)

In 1970, however, Asper placed his personal business plan on hold for a run at politics. New Democrat Edward Schreyer was in power in Manitoba, and Asper, never short of self-confidence, was sure he could topple the popular socialist and install a Liberal government in the province. He announced his intention of seeking the party leadership. John and Stuart Craig both attended the convention that chose Asper as leader. "He spoke very well, very enthusiastically," Stuart recalled. "After that, he was in our studio quite a bit as leader of the Liberal Party. I thought he was a very aggressive guy." Just how aggressive was to become painfully clear in the years to come.

Asper's political ambitions evaporated when the people handed him a drubbing at the polls in 1973. Schreyer's NDP waltzed back into power. The Liberals won only 5 of 57 legislature seats; Asper himself squeaked through in his own Winnipeg riding by only four votes. With their political future bleak, Asper and his top aide, Peter Liba, began casting about for options.

As the two would later retell the incident, one day in the summer of 1973 Liba was scanning the Winnipeg *Free Press* when he stumbled upon a notice inserted by the CRTC. It invited proposals for a third local television service in the city. Neither Liba nor his boss had any experience in broadcasting. But they had deep connections in the party that got to pick who sat on the CRTC. Moreover, in Asper they had a pitchman with a remarkable ability to conflate blue-sky aspiration with accomplished fact in the minds of his audience. For Izzy, as he admitted himself in the foreword to *The CanWest Global Story,* a self-published account of the company's first twenty years, there was never a moment's doubt that "you can make 2 + 2 equal 6."

What Asper and Liba lacked, however, was money. In a particularly ironic turn of events, it would be Stuart Craig who helped them find it.

In Brandon, Stu had been doing sums. He calculated that to put a station on the air in Winnipeg would cost about $1.7 million. He didn't have it. And while CKX could probably carry the load if he had to borrow it all, the right kind of partner with some equity to invest would be preferable. He put in a call to a fellow he knew in Winnipeg: Paul Morton, whose chain of Odeon movie theatres extended into

Brandon, where Morton had once considered buying a parcel of land Stuart owned for a cinema. Craig asked the Winnipeg man whether he would be interested in participating in a bid for the new TV licence—say, 10 to 15 per cent. Morton seemed warm to the idea and asked for a copy of Craig's application draft. Stuart agreed to provide it.

Morton took a look at the application and put in a call of his own—to Asper.

With Morton's money and show business connections on board, Asper and Liba rounded out their team by recruiting Seymour Epstein, a broadcast engineer and consultant from Toronto. Initially, Morton and Epstein would represent the application; the role of Liberal MLA and provincial party leader Asper would be downplayed, at least in public.

Together, the Winnipeg group determined on a proposal that would get them past their collective inexperience in the business of TV (Epstein's technical knowledge notwithstanding) at a single stroke. For some time, Winnipeg's two local stations (CKY and the local CBC affiliate, CBWT) had shared the market with an interloping signal from a station just south of the Canada–U.S. border in Pembina, North Dakota. The American station on Channel 12, like other stations in similar situations in Bellingham, Washington, and Buffalo, New York, made no bones about focussing its sales efforts on the Canadian city. In fact, KCND drew 95 per cent of its revenue from Winnipeg, where it maintained an active sales office.

In an appeal to patriotism that would become a mantra of future applications in which Asper was involved, the investors proposed to buy up KCND—lock, stock and transmitter—and move the whole thing to Canada. In one shot, the Asper-Liba-Morton-Epstein station would acquire an existing audience, an existing bank of sales accounts and an experienced station operator in Jerry Johnson, a Canadian-born broadcaster who was president of KCND. As a bonus, acquiring the Pembina outlet would (or so its backers argued) remove from the Winnipeg market a foreign competitor that had been draining Canadian dollars south of the border.

As it happened, the U.S. station's Texas-based billionaire owner, Gordon McLendon, had a motive for trying to unload his North Dakota asset at about that time. The Canadian government, prompted by broadcasters in Toronto and Vancouver as well as Winnipeg, was threatening to pass legislation disallowing advertising bought on cross-border stations as a tax-deductible business expense. The law would put KCND out of business overnight. McLendon agreed to sell if the Canadians got the licence they were seeking. It was Jerry Johnson who suggested the new Winnipeg station seek the Canadian call letters CKND to minimize the leakage of any audience loyal to its Pembina antecedent.

The CRTC called hearings to consider the applications for May 1974. By then a third bid, launched by an idealistic co-op group, was also in the ring. It was strong on enthusiasm and naively optimistic in its forecasts, and few observers gave it any serious chance. In Winnipeg business circles most people knew Morton; few knew Craig. Like many, Winnipeg *Tribune* business reporter Don Atkinson thought the CanWest application fronted by Morton was a shoo-in.

Until the day of the hearing, that is. "The real surprise," Atkinson wrote afterward, "was the sharp, thorough and well-presented submission by Western Manitoba Broadcasters Ltd." Stuart Craig, he added, delivered "by far the most polished of the presentations."

Atkinson wasn't the only one who was surprised by the imagination and quality of the WestMan application. In the CanWest camp, there was shock and dismay. "I went back to the hotel room and I was really sick about it," Johnson remembers. "They beat us hands-down. Particularly in the area of programming, they completely slaughtered us."

Johnson had been in a dilemma over CKND's programming proposals from the outset of the CanWest bid. His own instinct had been to develop a line-up that reflected the new station's supposed Canadian character. But Epstein, against Johnson's advice, had ordered him "to programme the station the way we were programming the U.S. station, with a large amount of American programming, and to largely disregard Canadian content," Johnson recalls. Johnson objected, but in the end, "they developed a program schedule with which I did not agree, but which I had to present."

In contrast to CanWest's schedule of warmed-over American series, WestMan proposed a schedule that leaned heavily on local news and information, and on programming developed by and for local community groups. "You know that a station must have equipment," Stuart told the CRTC panel. "But its biggest asset, if it's good, or its biggest liability, if it's bad, is its programming." In a particularly innovative move, WestMan's budget included funding for twenty-five Kodak film cameras that could be loaned to community organizations to produce their own programs.

Shaken, Morton and Epstein regrouped. Knowing that Johnson had gone ahead and developed a schedule of his own, they demanded he turn it over to them. Although it did not match WestMan's creativity, it did include significantly more Canadian content than CanWest's original proposals. The following day, the two men instructed Johnson to remain in his room while they returned to the CRTC hearings for the portion of the agenda known as "Replies," during which applicants get to respond to their competitors and, if they desire, clarify their own proposals. Blaming the all-American line-up on a lapse in judgement by the absent Johnson, Morton and Epstein presented his schedule as CanWest's revised programming plan.

As always, the CRTC reserved its decision. All three groups of applicants went home to nurse their nervousness. In the immaculate split-level on Cedar Bay, where most family conversation sooner or later returned to business, Shirley and Stuart guessed and second-guessed and triple-guessed what the federal regulator might do. Surely, they told themselves, the most experienced broadcaster with the best programming ideas would get the nod. With the boys, they even allowed themselves to discuss where they should live when they moved to Winnipeg.

It wasn't to be. Boyd, fourteen at the time, was at home when the decision reached Brandon late in 1974. "I remember when my dad phoned and told my mom that we didn't get the licence. It was just devastating. That set us back fifteen years."

There was a silver lining—of sorts. The CRTC had been unable to entirely ignore the merits of Stuart's application. Its ruling made that explicit: "The Commission was favourably impressed with Western Manitoba programming concepts," the ruling read, "and considers that an arrangement enabling it to participate in the ownership and direction of CanWest would be beneficial."

Paragraph seven of the decision stated:

> It is a condition of the Commission's approval of the CanWest application therefore that Western Manitoba be given an opportunity by CanWest to conclude an agreement which is subject to the Commission's approval to (A) acquire, either directly or indirectly, a significant number of the shares of CanWest and (B) participate in the management or direction of CanWest.

The commission's acknowledgement made a thin salve, however, for the sting of losing the licence. The condition it placed on CanWest's victory would turn into a cruel joke. The commission had instructed the parties to negotiate the CRTC requirement "in good faith." But the only proposals of substance that Morton and Epstein appeared willing to discuss involved no role for the Craigs in CanWest, either in management or in ownership. Quite the contrary: their idea was that CanWest should buy out the Craigs.

Once again, Stuart said no. This time it didn't take any thought at all.

KCND-TV, Pembina, went off the air on August 30, 1975. CKND-TV, Winnipeg, went on the air the next day. Within a year, a new stick stood on the concrete footings in North Dakota left vacant by the tower CanWest had dismantled and trucked to Canada. (It was eventually used to deliver CKND's signal to Asper's hometown of Minnedosa.) Another American station was beaming its signal into Winnipeg, although—on the orders of the CRTC—it would be banned from cable there.

For another dozen years, Stuart Craig's energies would be bottled up in Brandon. That wasn't such a bad thing. The boys were growing fast. Drew, in fact, joined CKX's staff just one month after CKND went to air. Meanwhile, there were other ventures to explore. Some would prove handsomely profitable over the next decade; others would frankly be for fun, or for the sake of the community. But his first brush with the group surrounding his contemporary from Minnedosa left Stuart Craig with a lasting and unfavourable impression of Izzy Asper.

Jerry Johnson questions how great a role Asper played in the execution of CanWest's 1974 application. He suggests Morton and Epstein had more to do with it. Even so, as soon as the handover from KC- to CKND was properly completed, the veteran broadcaster walked away from the trio. "I was convinced," he says, "that these people were not for me."

6

Family Business

If it was tough, over the years, having everyone in town know who your dad was and what he did for a living—and having many of them give you a hard time because he was keeping *their* dad from watching the Hamilton Tiger Cats rough up the Blue Bombers in the Grey Cup—there were perks to growing up a Craig kid. They didn't have much to do with money. Instead, they were the kind from which good memories and lasting ties spring.

There were the cartoons that Stuart would bring home, along with a projector, and show at birthday parties—an awesome hit in the days before home VCRs brought the *Lion King* into every six-year-old's bedroom. There was the mixed pleasure and embarrassment of going over to the station every year at Christmas to wrap presents—*on camera*— for the toy drive. There was the time the producers of *The Littlest Hobo,* a hugely popular Canadian series that followed the adventures of an itinerant German shepherd dog, came to Brandon on a promotional tour. The three Craig boys got to meet the show's star—only to be shocked to discover there was not one but *four* "littlest hobos."

Visits to the studios on Victoria Avenue were not frequent, but they were memorable. "There's a *smell,* a musty studio smell, that I just love," reflects Drew. The aroma—a confection created by too little ventilation, too many electronic whizmos turning air to ozone and, in the old days, stale tobacco smoke—is instantly recognizable to anyone who has ever smelled it. It became a sort of touchstone of the young Craigs's budding bond to broadcasting.

The business seeped into the growing family's consciousness in another way, too: it dominated the conversation between Stuart and Shirley the way other couples might share their passion for show dogs or Provençal cooking. It was the family hobby as well as its breadwinner. "I was born into the business of broadcasting," says Miles. "Dad used to tell us we had our boardroom meetings around the kitchen table." Sitting in front of the family TV, everyone joined to critique the station's news and commercials. At the same time, without quite realizing it, the boys were soaking up what might be considered the homeschooling equivalent of a business degree.

There was not much travel for the Craig boys. Apart from the conventions that John and Stuart Craig had always attended, as would the next generation, as a valuable means of keeping attuned to the industry's drumbeat, there was little time and not really the means for extended vacation travel. "Occasionally we'd drive into Winnipeg," remembers Boyd of his childhood years. "That was always a big thing. I thought it was this big, big city! We thought they had great radio stations."

There were long and priceless summers up at the lake, though. Every June at the end of school, Shirley and the boys would move house to the cottage on Clear Lake, returning to Brandon just in time for Labour Day and the new academic year. The sun-filled, sand-filled, rainy-day-and-cards-filled days seemed to go on forever.

One summer, Drew met the woman with whom he would fall in love. Jodi Rutledge's family was also in broadcasting: her grandfather owned a part interest in radio station CKDM in Dauphin, Manitoba. The Rutledges had a cabin near the Craigs's in the poplar and cedar woods that run back from the lake into the heart of Riding Mountain National Park. "We kind of grew up together on Clear Lake," Drew remembers. "Jodi used to fix me up with her girlfriends. One day the lightbulb finally went on." The two married in December 1983.

Stuart "never really encouraged us to get involved" in the family business, Drew recalls. "He said, 'Get out of here. Go get your education and then come and see me.'" But in Drew's case at least, the admonition was idle. Johnny Craig's lanky eldest grandson already knew where he wanted to end up. "I just fell in love with the business," he says. "I used to spend a lot more time [at the station] than my dad knew about."

In September 1974 at age seventeen, Drew Craig went to work part-time for CKX-TV, fitting evenings and weekends at the station around his Grade 12 homework. His first job, like his father's, was one that one nobody else wanted: servicing a vast and cranky stainless-steel, military-duty, 16-mm film processor Stuart had picked up when Canada scrapped its only aircraft carrier, the HMCS *Bonaventure*, in 1967. Designed to process film from surveillance aircraft during war at sea, the dinner-table-sized machine could doubtless have survived a nuclear attack. But it was a cussed thing to use. Film had to be loaded into the beast in total darkness, and its innards, where the film was "souped," were temperamental. When the job was not done right, there were no pictures for the six o'clock news, let alone "film at eleven." It was a task everyone was glad to pass on to the boss's son. (It is a powerful indicator of the pace of technological change in broadcasting that the film universally used for TV reportage in 1975 has since been supplanted by new technologies not once but twice: first by videotape and then by digital recordings.)

After a while, Drew got to go on the road—shooting sports footage of weekend bonspiels all over the western prairie, then driving the film back to Brandon to process. After two years of university, Drew's hours at the station shifted to full-time. Stuart made sure, as he would for all his sons, that there was as little chance as possible for nepotism. "He handed us off to one of the managers," says Drew, "who probably thought, 'Here's the boss's kid. Let's put him through his paces.' We paid our dues."

Lawrence Dubois, CKX's long-standing chief engineer, now retired, confirms that diplomatically. "Stuart'd certainly go after them if something wasn't done; he'd want to know why. They had some very good discussions," Dubois says, with a meaningful tilt of an eyebrow. "And they listened."

Boyd Craig's transit into broadcasting would begin within a year of his brother's but take almost a decade longer to complete. In October 1976, at sixteen, he began working weekend relief in CKX Radio's master control room—a job that entailed mainly loading and cueing audio tapes and tape cartridges, then playing them in the order dictated by the printed traffic log sheet. After finishing high school in 1978, however, the middle Craig son set out to try his hand at higher education. But neither a season at the University of Manitoba in Winnipeg nor a stretch at the University of British Columbia truly engaged his interest. By the end of 1980, Boyd was back in Brandon. For a while he returned to the station, writing radio ads. "The person in charge of the creative department made me stay at night to learn to type," he says. But he still questioned whether the family business was for him.

Miles had fewer doubts. "I always thought I would get into broadcasting eventually," the youngest Craig son says. Like his older brothers, he cut his teeth on the station's "joe jobs"—shooting and processing still photos for TV, switching the Winnipeg Jets games that were broadcast on FM, running a camera as summer relief. But Miles seemed to have the academic bent that had bypassed his older brothers: he got the best marks of any of them in high school. After graduating in 1979, Miles moved to Winnipeg to study commerce at the University of Manitoba, rooming with a succession of friends from Brandon. In 1983 he graduated with an Honours Bachelor of Commerce degree and a major in finance.

Unwinding at Clear Lake after his final university year, Miles and a similarly unemployed buddy were looking for a way to make some money when one day they noticed something. "It became obvious to us that the garbage-can stands at all the cottages were in need of replacing," he remembers. "So we came up with a design, and our summer job was building and selling garbage-can stands."

Frustrated for the time being in his desire to break out of his quiet corner of southwestern Manitoba, Stuart Craig extended WestMan's reach wherever he could. Through Relay, he did a creative deal to deliver local programming to the area around Dauphin, Manitoba's fourth-largest community, 140 kilometres north of Brandon. The arrangement gave Dauphin a daily news show and other local productions on an existing CBC network rebroadcaster, in return for the local advertising. In 1981, CKX added another "rebroad" on the eastern perimeter of Riding Mountain Park.

And he got involved in other ventures. When the fabled Brandon Wheat Kings threatened to fold, Stu joined seven other businessmen (among them Bob Cornell) to rescue Johnny Craig's former team. "We felt it was important for the community. They'd always had a hockey team," he explained later. "It took a couple of years to get it turned around, but we did." The consortium sold the team, now solvent, to its manager. But "he proceeded to screw the whole thing up again," Stuart recalled. "So Cornell and I went back in and bought it, the two of us. It didn't take very long, and we had it turned around again and it was making money." This time Stu sold his shares to Cornell—at cost.

The Wheat Kings had been for fun, and for Brandon's sporting pride. But Craig and Cornell enjoyed doing business with one another. Soon they, with another local man, Glen Fowler, who owned the town Chrysler dealership, were partners in a semi-hobby development business. Starting with forty acres of land that Craig had acquired in 1972 to put up the tower that broadcast CKX's signal, the group eventually amassed over a hundred acres. After putting in roads and services, they sold lots to local builders. The trick, they quickly learned, was "You don't service too far ahead."

Then one of the *tres amigos* heard about a parcel of land becoming available in Scottsdale, Arizona. A former horse warm-up track with room for 301 lots in the heart of one of America's pre-eminent retirement towns was on the market for US$3.5 million. In a kind of business-boys'-night-out atmosphere, "nothing would do," recalled Stuart, "but we'd go down and service them up." The trio started to do just that, but it was the early 1980s, and before they could hit their stride, interest rates spiked. The three Canadians bailed out regretfully. "If we had got that thing going, we'd still be down there," Stu reflected. "There were so many opportunities."

But the land development business was always more of a lark than a love affair for Stuart. "We did it for fun," says Cornell. "I don't think anybody got very rich." Craig, his friend says, "really enjoyed getting away from his own type of business." On at least one occasion, there may have been a wee bit too *much* fun. During one business trip to the Arizona project, Fowler's wife received a call from a suspicious FBI agent. What exactly, he wanted to know, were several million dollars' worth of credit letters doing in a briefcase bearing Fowler's name that someone had found at the Scottsdale airport? The briefcase, it turned out, had been left behind after the three holidaying investors enjoyed one refreshment too many at the airport bar.

On his own, Craig also began to profit from land he had accumulated over time around CKX's studio buildings in Brandon. In the years since his father had acquired two city blocks of open prairie for the new station in 1955, Stuart had added as much again to the land holding. With Brandon's expansion over the same period, the property was no longer out of town: instead, it was prime commercial and residential real estate. Stuart began to let some of it go and to develop other parcels. Eventually, he would build a retail and office mall on a lot next door to the station. For a time, he was even in the hotel business. When the Royal Oak Inn, a block west of the CKX studios on Victoria Avenue (which is also Highway 1A), came up for sale in the early eighties, Craig tapped some of his land development profits to acquire the establishment.

In 1982, he bought a second hotel. North Hill Inn stood on one of the two main routes into downtown Brandon from the Trans-Canada

Highway and boasted a 150-seat restaurant, a 400-seat banquet room and a 250-seat nightclub. Stu thought the hotel had potential, but it was struggling. So, in a different way, was young Boyd. His academic interests tapped out, Boyd was looking for something to do. Stuart put him in charge of the North Hill Inn. "Three weeks in the kitchen and two weeks as a waiter ... that was my training to be manager of the hotel," Boyd laughs in retrospect. "I didn't have a clue!" He was twenty-two.

There were some false starts. A lavish renovation of the restaurant and nightclub soaked up a million dollars before Boyd concluded it was a failure. And in a scene straight out of *It's a Wonderful Life,* the younger Craig once mislaid the club's cash receipts for a period of several desperate hours. But within nine months, the North Hill was beginning to generate a positive return on the family's investment. Under Boyd's management, the hotel rang up the highest gross liquor sales of any cabaret-licenced establishment in Manitoba. Indeed, it was in danger of becoming *too* successful: it was sometimes difficult to make the 20 per cent minimum of receipts that the liquor licensing board rules required be for food orders.

It was about then, with the North Hill Inn beginning to tick along nicely on its own, that Boyd Craig lost interest. "I just got sick of it," he says. In 1985, he rejoined CKX's staff in the sales department—and promptly drew the least desirable account. His territory was the diaspora of small rural hamlets with names like Souris and Hartney, Hamiota and Killarney, that fill the bottom left-hand corner of the Manitoba map. Most have no more than a couple of thousand residents, and many struggle hard to avoid becoming ghost towns in the slow seeping away of country folk toward the city. It was rare to find a retailer who could afford a television ad of his or her own. So instead, Boyd came up with the idea of selling entire *towns* a commercial praising their civic amenities—tagged with the names of the local retail sponsors, mentioned in rotation. "It took three or four months," he remembers, "but then I was making some decent cash. At least, decent to me."

Two more attempts to win television licences in Winnipeg had been rebuffed. In 1983, the Craigs had decided that if they couldn't expand into the broadcast side of home entertainment, perhaps there was opportunity in the consumer end. That autumn, under Miles's management, they opened Video Connection, a large home-electronics and video-rental retail store. It was almost instantly profitable, and the store soon branched out into the personal computers that were just beginning to hit the home and small-business markets. As the first retailer in the area to carry Macintosh machines, Miles acquired an early appreciation of the usefulness of spread-sheet accounting and other computer-assisted management tasks. He soon began to integrate computers into other Craig businesses. (The family later closed the store and liquidated its inventory, after deciding "we didn't want to be in that business," says Miles. As new horizons opened up in broadcasting, he notes, "it was taking up too much time.")

For all the joy and satisfaction that Stuart Craig took in his sons' growing accomplishments, by the early 1980s another close relationship was causing mainly anguish.

As the decade began, Johnny Craig's age was beginning to tell. Long gone were the star goalie's lightning reflexes and even, more often than not, the natural salesman's quick wit. For John Craig's daughter Catherine, it was heartbreaking to see the father she once thought of as "the smartest man I've ever known" slip into forgetfulness and disorientation. Increasingly, Doreen Craig did her travelling alone or with a woman friend, leaving John at home. During those absences, it was Shirley who made certain her father-in-law was well cared for.

On December 15, 1980, his second wife placed John Craig in Brandon's Central Park nursing home, directly across the street from the television station he had founded. The following July, Doreen Craig secured an order from a Winnipeg judge declaring her husband incompetent and naming her as "committee"—in English, trustee—of his affairs.

His family did not contest that John was no longer able to manage his business interests, but they were shocked by Doreen's sweeping and pre-emptive assumption of his affairs. Moreover, the two psychiatric reports she had filed to support her application to have John committed were out of date. She had failed to notify the public trustee, as required by Manitoba's Mental Health Act, at least ten days before seeking the judge's declaration. And she had neglected to tell the judge that John had two very concerned children living in Brandon. Nevertheless, the order putting John Craig's affairs in Doreen's hands was to stand for nearly two and a half years.

It did not take Doreen, who knew how to read a balance sheet as well as any businessperson, long to discover that her husband did not, in fact, own any shares in CKX. According to memos on the station's ownership filed with the CRTC, the last shares had been transferred to Stuart in 1977. What she considered worse news followed. Less than thirty days after Doreen had Johnny Craig declared incompetent, Stuart and Catherine, the only other directors of J. B. Craig Investments Ltd., repository of the small remains of their father's capital that had survived his second wife's spending habits, voted to remove their father as its president.

Three and a half months after seizing control of her husband's affairs, Doreen sued his children. Stuart and Catherine promptly countersued.

The court actions would drag on for seven years and wend their way to the Manitoba Court of Appeal three times before finally being settled. A 1983 appeal court ruling did, however, withdraw Doreen's status as "committee" over John's affairs and placed them in the care of the public trustee. The move somewhat eased the Craig family's distress. But for the rest of her father's life, Catherine says with evident resentment, "every pair of pants we bought for him, every pair of socks, had to go to the 'committee' in Winnipeg."

Until the last year of Johnny Craig's life, however, Stuart made sure that his father was able to spend at least a few days each summer at his beloved Clear Lake.

A truce in Stuart Craig's legal battle with his stepmother was still some way off in 1985, when a chain of events began that would finally repay all the frustration and disappointment he had suffered in his attempts to break Western Manitoba Broadcasters free of its small-town market. Once again, the CRTC invited applications for a television station in Manitoba, this time to employ the last unoccupied off-air VHF channel in the province that was capable of serving Winnipeg, Channel 13.

In Brandon, there was consensus among the Craigs that there was no minimizing the importance of the licence to the family company. "If we didn't get out of this small market," Boyd knew as well as anyone, "we weren't going to be in broadcasting much longer." So the Craigs determined to try something a little different. Their proposal would still commit to substantial amounts of local programming. But they would try to disarm the inevitable squawks of protest from Winnipeg's incumbent private broadcasters—Moffat and CanWest—by "going in through the back door," as Stu put it—seeking a licence for Portage la Prairie instead of Winnipeg proper.

At a hearing early in 1986, Moffat and CanWest, as expected, intervened against WestMan's third application, objecting that another TV station in Winnipeg would drain off more revenue than they could afford. But this time around two things were different.

The Craigs—for the first time, Drew and Miles joined Stuart at the hearing table—promised that their new Portage la Prairie station, if licensed, would refrain from seeking or accepting any "retail" (locally purchased) advertising from sponsors in the larger city.

And there was another factor at work. Izzy Asper, by now front and centre in CanWest's executive suite, had been vocal—*highly* vocal—about the immense amounts of money his operation was making. As a result, in Stuart's view, "Although they were saying there was no room for us in Winnipeg, people didn't believe it." On May 8, 1986, the CRTC approved Western Manitoba Broadcasters' application.

Stuart Craig had finally gotten his ticket out of Brandon. Eventually, he and his sons would ride it to the edge of the national stage. But first it would almost bankrupt them.

Above: The first advertisers on television delivered their message wherever they could, even putting their products in front of announcers like sportscaster Henry Stothard.

Left: The CKX-TV broadcast stage at the Manitoba Exhibition, inaugurated in 1958, pioneered the live television remote and quickly became one of the annual fair's most popular attractions.

CKX·TV
CHANNEL 5

Above: Spotlight on Talent was one of several ongoing series that CKX Television produced during the late 1950s and into the 1960s.

Right: Another show instructed viewers in the newly popular hobby of back-yard barbecuing.

Above: Live commercials could end in disaster if a sponsor forgot his lines.

Above: Reach for the Top pitted local high-school teams against each other in knowledge-testing quizzes.

Right: In the 1950s, sponsor T. Eaton Co. still ran a mail-order business popular with rural Manitobans.

Below: Tobacco advertising, later banned, here pays for an election night broadcast.

CKX-TV
GENERAL ELECTRIC

Left: John and Stuart Craig are shown here examining a new transmitter that increased CKX Television's broadcast signal strength in 1962. Later, "rebroadcast" transmitters extended the station's reach to remote parts of the province.

Below: A contractor's mistake during the erection of a new, 185-metre television antenna in the spring of 1961 triggered the collapse of the incomplete tower, tragically killing two workers.

John Craig's grandsons, *(left to right)* Boyd, Drew and Miles Craig, visited the CKX-TV studios in the mid-sixties to meet the multiple canine stars of the popular Canadian series *The Littlest Hobo.*

7

Skirmishes

There are two ways to get into broadcasting, as in most businesses. You buy in—the path Asper, Morton and Epstein's CanWest largely adopted—or you build. The Craigs have always been builders.

There are upsides to that. If a new broadcasting station—radio or television—finds its audience, its value can quickly multiply to many times the initial investment. If that first flirtation with viewers flowers into a full-blown relationship, the product is a franchise with the potential to spin profit almost in perpetuity. A sterling example of the latter is the extraordinary hold that CHAN-TV, better known to its Vancouver viewers as BCTV, has over that market's evening news hour. In a city served by four local and one neighbouring city station (CHEK-TV, Victoria), BCTV in the 1990s regularly commanded news-hour audience shares of more than 60 per cent, a position of such dominance that some social pundits accused it of single-handedly driving British Columbia's political agenda.

But there are risks to being builders, and they are all on the front end.

In many respects, the commitment to build and put to air a brand-new, free service, off-air television station is an act of faith every bit as irrational as the one portrayed in the film *Field of Dreams.* "Build it and they will come" pretty accurately describes the optimistic assumption of a new television enterprise as well, with the difference that a TV station is many, many times more expensive than a set of bleachers in a cornfield.

As much as a million dollars may go into the application alone. The modern document is a genetically altered, steroid-bulked-up version of the concise forms that represented the first pioneering television proposals. Today's application to the CRTC is expected to include social surveys to show that audiences are panting for the types of programs being proposed. Market studies, to demonstrate that demand for TV advertising exceeds what is available from "incumbent" broadcasters and that the anguished wails over the prospect of revenue lost to the new kid on the block are so many alligator tears. Explanations at length of the benefits—the *incremental* benefits—that will flow to Canadian culture from the new outlet, in return for its use of the public's radio spectrum. Evidence, in the form of letters of support, briefs and interventions, to show that key community, artistic and industry constituencies view the new station as a boon, not a predator. To say nothing of detailed forecasts confiding to the commission the most intimate expectations of the applicant's financial plan.

Then you get the licence, and the *real* spending begins. Studio space. Tower location. Hardware: not only the steel lacework of the tower and the humming, high-voltage cabinets of the transmitter, but microwave and satellite dishes, and the increasingly complex requirements of a well-equipped television production and switching centre. People. Programs. The inevitable catalogue of telephones and fax machines, chairs and cabinets, water coolers and credenzas without which the contemporary office worker is unable to function.

As the Craigs watched the bills mount for the new service they planned to call the Manitoba Television Network (MTN), their blood chilled. One day in the autumn of 1986, Shirley visited the Portage la Prairie studios. Truckloads of new furniture and electronic equipment arrived almost hourly. Thoroughly familiar with WestMan's balance sheet, she looked on aghast as item after item was checked off the order list. "We're going to have to send that back!" she finally erupted. "Where are we going to get the money to pay for it?'"

Drew, who became the new station's founding general manager at the age of twenty-eight, concedes: "The projected losses [from MTN] were far more significant than we ever anticipated. That is as close as we've ever come as a company to getting into serious trouble."

As everyone in the family knew, the advertising order book that was supposed to underwrite all the shiny new facilities was virtually blank. It was partly the consequence of the Craigs's own impatience to be up and running by mid-October 1986. Many local advertisers didn't think the on-air date was realistic and refused to buy time in the early weeks of MTN's schedule. Most national media buyers, meanwhile, had already made their commitments for campaigns scheduled to air during the new station's first autumn.

There were other reasons for the dearth of early advertising sales.

The television market, in Manitoba's capital and elsewhere, was going through a transition. New services were delivering all-sports, all-news, all-movie and music-video channels to the large majority of urban homes subscribing to cable. By the late eighties, the so-called "specialty channel" share of cable audiences approached 30 per cent. Local broadcasters continued to dominate the remaining audience, but the specialty services had drawn off a considerable share of major national sponsorship. "The Coca-Colas and the Labatts began to spend on TSN and other cable services instead of on off-the-air broadcasters," recalls Ken Clark, a veteran TV executive from the Maritimes who became general manager of the Moffat station in Winnipeg in 1989.

It was during the 1980s as well that entertainment spending, especially among the young, first began to show the impact of the mass-market microchip. During that decade, personal VCRs and video games, both at home and in the arcades, began to attract significant consumer spending. They would prove to be only outriders of the avalanche of choices that would flow from the fertile marriage of fantasy and microengineering in the 1990s: Myst, chat rooms, web surfing and e-shopping. But already, they dampened the historic growth of audiences for conventional television.

Taken together, these factors fuelled bitter competition for television ad sales. With four local Canadian stations and a reconstituted border station (a successor to the KCND station that CanWest had undertaken to remove from the field) beaming their signals into Winnipeg, the city became the battlefield for a price war. "Nobody would stick to their rate card," recalls CKY's Clark, "and the national advertisers would just knock the price down as much as they could." During the second half of the 1980s, the value of air time in Winnipeg would grow at only a fraction of the pace of other centres.

And then there was the self-imposed sacrifice the Craigs had offered: forgoing retail advertising from the city of Winnipeg. True, Portage la Prairie offered some local advertising, but with 14,000 people, it was even smaller than Brandon. There would be a shot at some national buys once the station could demonstrate through ratings that it had an audience. But the big prize—the retail advertising supported by Winnipeg's 680,000 people—remained off limits. "We were looking through the window into the market," Drew Craig laments.

The younger Craigs, in fact, were far from happy with the restriction and had argued about it with their father, during the licence application as well as afterward. It was an expensive commitment. But in Stuart's mind, it was partly a question of equity. The Moffats had stepped aside to give WestMan the opportunity, through Relay Communications, to profit from CKY's entry into Brandon. Even though CKY wasn't the only player in Winnipeg, Stu felt, "It wouldn't be fair to go into Winnipeg and start selling retail." Besides, he told his boys, "I don't think we'd have ever gotten the licence without [the commitment]." Still, it hurt.

It further crimped revenues that Relay itself had been wound up on MTN's launch. CKY continued to extend a wholesale rate to CKX salespeople on its Brandon avails. But the "beautiful deal" was over.

The question of MTN's access to Winnipeg retail sales would simmer for the better part of a decade. With the station losing money badly, the younger Craigs would override Stuart's objections in 1990 and file an emergency request with the CRTC to be relieved of the licence condition. The commission dismissed the application. Boyd, who had pressed hard for the emergency appeal, weighed the blemish to the family's reputation for fulfilling licence commitments to the letter and concluded: "Stu was right." The condition was continued when the CRTC renewed MTN's licence in 1991, but it was dropped when the licence was renewed a second time, in 1995.

Meanwhile, though, as the time came for MTN to buy its second season of programming, the Craig's break-out station was straining and scraping for every penny of revenue. Then, from a familiar quarter, came another blow. "Our friends at CanWest," recalls Drew, "decided they were going to try to give us a hard time in terms of buying programs." What cash-rich CanWest actually did was to buy rights to twice as many U.S.-produced programs as it needed for the following year's schedule—effectively shutting the Craigs out of the bidding for many of the hit American shows that are the bedrock of most Canadian commercial television schedules. (CKY and CBWT, on the other hand, were beneficiaries of CTV and CBC network buys.) "In our second year of operation, we had nothing. It devastated us," Drew says simply.

Operating from instinct, analysis of the options and a measure of desperation, Drew Craig began buying up Manitoba broadcast rights to movies. He built a new season schedule from scratch out of local programming and prime-time feature films. And he held his breath.

Back in Brandon, Boyd moved into the assistant general manager's office next door to Stuart's. It was the office Drew had vacated when he and Jodi left to take over MTN. Boyd stepped into the role in time to witness the alarming outflow of funds from CKX to the new venture. “For a while there,” he says, “it looked like a real dumb decision ... because we lost *so* much money. It lost serious cash for two years, maybe three.” It didn’t help at all that CKX Radio, the business that had started it all for the family forty years earlier, was also losing money—along with most of the rest of the Canadian radio industry in the late eighties.

And then things got worse.

In 1989, the Communications, Energy and Paperworkers Union of Canada launched an organizing drive across the entire Manitoba broadcasting industry. With broadcasting struggling to trim expenses in a soft advertising market, the union found fertile ground for its campaign. Moffat’s CKY became the object of a bitter strike that dragged on through a Winnipeg winter from October to May.

Then the union came to Brandon. “I was like, ‘Yeah!’” says Lori Truscott, a radio reporter at CKX at the time. She quickly became an advocate of the union’s cause and helped it sign up the necessary number of employees to win certification. Recruitment was made easier by “the conditions that drive most people to unionize,” she says: poor pay and inequitable working conditions.

The Brandon outlet had long accepted its place in the broadcasting firmament as a “training station,” the sort of outfit where young talents pick up enough skills to compile an impressive audition tape, then move on to bigger markets. As such, it paid wages that were some distance from the top of the industry scale. And the management style handed down from the days of Johnny Craig’s firm hand struck younger employees like Truscott as being abrasively “old school: it was their way or the highway. As a result, a lot of people took the highway.”

The union was correct, moreover, in believing that the Craigs were holding off on purchasing new equipment at CKX in order to keep the lights on at MTN. While thriftiness with serviceable gear is admirable, the union tapped into an additional source of grumbling that, as Truscott put it, “some of the equipment [at CKX] was older than the people using it.”

The union drive appears to have involved little personal animosity toward the station’s owners. Truscott remembers one newly hired disc jockey who, in some consternation, recounted the following story: Wandering the still-unfamiliar station halls, he had run into a “friendly old guy." The two chatted for some time before the new on-air personality asked, "And what do you do around here?" The old guy answered: "I own the place."

Still, for the family, it was hard not to feel a sense of betrayal. It was Boyd who negotiated the difficult first contract with the union. "That was pure hell," he remembers. "My dad had no use for unions. He took it very personally . . . and I had to go in there and negotiate. I remember the day I gave them vision care—I got such shit for that." But the decision stood. Stuart Craig might disagree with his sons' judgements, but he would not overrule them. In 1990, at the end of exhausting negotiations that went down to the last few hours before a strike deadline, WestMan and the Communications, Energy and Paperworkers Union reached a collective agreement. The union members voted to accept the contract (renewed several times since without incident).

In retrospect, Drew Craig calls the unionization "a natural process: you go from a Mom-and-Pop shop to a larger entity." But at the same time, he says, "It was a personal blow to us. It's a hard pill to swallow for a lot of entrepreneurs. And it is never quite the same in terms of the relationship."

Beset both at home and in Portage la Prairie, Stuart Craig turned to his hole cards: the two now-thriving Brandon hotels he had acquired. It was a difficult decision to cut them loose, but at the end of the day he was a broadcaster, not a hotelier. With regret, Craig put North Hill and then the Royal Oak Inn on the market. "I regret sometimes that we sold the Royal Oak Inn," Stu reflected later. "It was the best hotel in Brandon—still is. But we were starting MTN and losing money there, so we decided to dump out of the hotel business."

The money went straight into the family's gamble on Winnipeg.

As the eighties came to a close, the new station began at last to turn around. More than turn around. The Craigs's bet on movies and local programming started to pay off in a big way. "Our input costs went down," Drew grins, "and our audience grew." Advertisers began to take notice—and to book time. By 1990, the new station was paying down its debt and beginning to contribute nicely to WestMan's bottom line.

But Drew would not quickly forget the lessons of Winnipeg. "It was good for learning how to operate in a *very* competitive market."

The company, and the Craigs, had been through a trial by fire. They had survived intact and strengthened. As the crisis receded, it became obvious too that, without much discussion, the family had successfully begun a second generational transition. Stuart Craig would remain very much an active participant in the company's management. But it was equally clear that his sons would henceforth speak with full authority for the company. It was becoming apparent where their respective strengths and talents lay.

Drew had piloted MTN through its troubled infancy. He was the rare television executive who really *did* know the business from the ground up. After a decade of shadowing his father at broadcast conventions and program-buying meetings, he was impressively well connected in the industry. And in Jodi, Drew seemed fortunate to have found the same kind of close professional and romantic partnership that Stuart had with Shirley. In the years before MTN, Drew and Jodi had produced an exercise series called *F.I.T.* at CKX's Brandon studios; dark-haired Jodi was its host. The series had sold in a more than a dozen U.S. markets and across Canada, making a significant contribution to West-Man's profits at the time. Now Jodi was deeply involved in programming at the new station. That role was interrupted in 1990, so that she could deliver the couple's first child, Dillon.

Two months after the birth of Johnny Craig's first great-grandchild, Boyd married the girl he had dated on and off since high school. Krista Einarson came from Icelandic stock; Icelanders were one of the many groups that had taken advantage of Clifford Sifton's Open-the-West policy. She had the blonde hair and easy self-confidence of that matrilineal culture's womenfolk. Boyd had noticed her first when he was in Grade 10 and she was in Grade 8. When their first child was born on July 1, 1991, she received an Icelandic name: Jonina, pronounced "*Yo*-nina."

Stuart and Shirley's second son was taking charge of an aspect of the expanding broadcast operation that had been somewhat neglected in the full-court press on Winnipeg. "As a family," Boyd concedes, "we hadn't put the effort into radio that we had into TV." And everywhere in the 1980s, radio had been going through a bad patch. Many stations were losing money. FM was just beginning to emerge from a decade and a half as the "poor sister" of many AM-FM operations, but it was not yet contributing much to earnings. "TV was running on its own, but our radio station was losing money like crazy," Boyd says. "And every time we tried something, it got worse. I took it on myself to get involved."

And if Drew was the brother who kept television content and audience points at his fingertips, Boyd Craig was emerging as the rainmaker and financial conscience of the company. His skills there may have derived in part from those early days of MTN's existence when, from his office next door to Stuart's, "I was the one who heard every day how much money we were losing. I didn't appreciate it."

Miles Craig had also been involved in getting MTN off the ground. After its launch, he moved to Portage la Prairie and settled in as the station's assistant manager. On the side, he worked to develop a visionary idea that Stuart had pursued for years: distributing cable-style TV directly to viewers' homes by microwave.

On May 6, 1991, a brief press release was faxed to business editors across Manitoba. Western Manitoba Broadcasters of Brandon, owner of CKX Radio and Television and of CHMI-TV, was changing its name. It would henceforth be known as Craig Broadcast Systems Inc. It's hard to say how many of those editors realized that, in their understated way, the boys from Brandon were throwing down their gloves and getting ready to rumble.

8

Golden Foothills

Ken Clark left the executive suite at Moffats's CKY-TV, Winnipeg, in February 1992 to take the reins of a new television network in New Zealand. Before his departure, however, the Maritimer conducted a critical piece of market research. He determined how much money advertisers had been willing to pay TV stations in Manitoba in 1985 for each "rating point" of audience (each rating point represents 1 per cent of the televisions available for viewing at that time of day within the market served) and compared it to what they were willing to pay in 1990. Then he did the same calculation for stations in Alberta. What he discovered was enough to make Manitoba broadcasters go green with envy.

At the start of the period, audience rating points had been worth about the same amount in both provinces: approximately $17. The dollars-per-rating-point comparison—as good a measure as any of the growth in earnings capacity of the stations involved—showed that over the five years in his study, the value of air time in Winnipeg had risen approximately 17 per cent, to about $20. In Alberta, it had shot up by 341 per cent—to $75 per rating point.

Clark's inquiry would have an unintended and ironic consequence. Acting on one of its former general manager's conclusions—that the Winnipeg market was undervalued as a result of excessive price competition—CKY in 1994 merged its local ad sales effort with that of its erstwhile rival, CanWest's CKND, forming a common sales team known as Total Marketing Group. But the effort to reduce competition backfired. The creation of a common marketing front prompted the CRTC to do what several appeals by the Craigs had failed to accomplish. The following year, the commission gave MTN the green light to sell retail ads in Winnipeg—in direct competition with CKY and CKND.

But Ken Clark had also uncovered hard evidence of something most broadcasters already knew in their guts: in the penultimate decade of the century, the eastern foothills of the Rockies were *the* place in Canada to make money on TV. "The awesomely profitable Alberta TV system, the most profitable in all of Canada" was how Wendell Wilks, a veteran broadcast executive from the province, described it in 1990. According to industry-wide figures published by Statistics Canada, the twelve stations licensed for Alberta had shared annual after-tax profits of up to $24 million between 1985 and 1990. By 1993, the weekly *Alberta Report* would estimate the industry's profits at $40 million a year.

In practice, the lion's share of that revenue went to only four stations based in Edmonton and Calgary: two CTV-affiliates, and two independent private stations. The CBC sold national network time on its Alberta stations, but it had bowed out of local retail sales in Calgary—the more lucrative market of the two—in 1990, in order to comply with CRTC policy after closing its studios in the city. The majority of the other "stations" recognized by Statistics Canada were in fact only rebroadcasters of Edmonton- and Calgary-originated signals.

Most of the Alberta stations had once been locally owned and operated. Now, none of the top four had its head office in the province. WIC Western International Communications Ltd. of Vancouver owned both independent stations: CITV-TV in Edmonton (acquired from its founder, Dr. Charles Allard, in 1990) and, in Calgary, CKKX-TV (formerly CFAC-TV, part of the now-extinct Selkirk chain; later rechristened CICT-TV by WIC, to match the "I"-for-Independent branding of the Edmonton station).

In 1996, Baton Broadcasting Systems Inc., the empire built on John Bassett's CFTO-TV in Toronto, had acquired the Calgary CTV affiliate, CFCN-TV, which had been founded by Gordon Love in the 1960s and operated by Maclean Hunter for a decade and a half. The other CTV outlet in the province, CFRN-TV Edmonton, belonged to Electrohome Ltd., a Kitchener, Ontario, company with interests in radio and a background in manufacturing electronics; that station had once belonged to the family of *its* founder, Dick Rice.

With only three local television services, Alberta—with twice the population—had fewer choices of hometown TV than Manitoba.

It wasn't only viewers who were affected. In fact, TV audiences may have been the folks *least* likely to notice how underserved the Alberta marketplace had become. Most of the top U.S. shows found a home somewhere on the local dial, even for those viewers not on cable. As for the additional local programming that might have existed in a more competitive market, what wasn't on offer wasn't missed.

The constraints were more noticeable in the business world, especially to anyone trying to buy advertising in Calgary or Edmonton. Quite simply, the demand for television advertising in Alberta far outstripped "avails"—the holes in the program day into which commercials could be inserted. "It takes me three times as long to buy Alberta compared to the rest of the country," one national ad agency director told Bay Consulting Group, a Toronto firm that Craig Broadcast hired to prepare an independent assessment of the Alberta market. "There isn't enough inventory."

The inequity in air-time supply and demand, moreover, gave Alberta's existing TV operators a leverage in relations with media buyers that they used relentlessly to ratchet up prices. "The existing stations," another media buyer complained to Bay Consulting in early 1993, "consistently try to jam through very high cost increases. Recently I had to deal with a double-digit increase compared to a year ago." Like many of her colleagues, that ad buyer concluded: "I would strongly welcome an additional channel in Alberta."

In Brandon, the Craigs were eager to provide one. But so were others.

One of those vying to get into the gate was Wendell Wilks. The Albertan had helped Allard launch his Edmonton independent station, CITV-TV, in the early 1970s, but since the mid-1980s had been pursuing the quixotic dream of a service of his own, which he dubbed ATN, "The Alberta Television Network." Despite years of effort and numerous appearances before the CRTC, Wilks's enterprise by 1993 still consisted, in Calgary *Herald* television columnist Bob Blakey's words, of "a legal entity, some business cards and an office on a sprawling industrial lot."

Wilks's dreams were much more expansive, involving TV stations in the province's two largest cities as well as a huge, $600-million production centre in Calgary that was to be integrated into a theme park *à la* Florida's MGM World. But Wilks's proposals had been hampered over the years by his inflammatory style, an ill-concealed resentment at the frustration of his dreams and an often bitterly argued Alberta chauvinism. In objecting to WIC's acquisition of CFAC-TV during one CRTC hearing, Wilks accused the Vancouver company of dropping a "poison pill" on his province, stripping out television profits while leaving behind "scorched earth." Rumbled Wilks: "Now all of our major media are branch plants in this province. We Albertans have to go cup in hand to Vancouver for our decisions. Do you think Quebecers would stand for such a situation? Would Ontario?"

When the CRTC, in 1993, issued a call for proposals to establish a fourth television service in Alberta, Wilks, like an old cavalryman who hears the distant note of the bugle, saddled up for one more fight.

Chauvinism of a different sort would be the leitmotif of another, more dangerous rival.

By submitting an unsolicited application early in 1993, it was Izzy Asper's CanWest that prompted the commission to issue a call for licence proposals in Alberta. (CanWest's initial proposal had been withdrawn after the CRTC's call and replaced with an updated one.) Throughout the licence play, CanWest, with its congenitally hyperconfident CEO, would act—and sometimes speak—as though the application process were a mere formality. Asper's tireless lobbying (he haunted the provincial legislature during its 1993 sitting) and public statements, in which he cloaked CanWest's pursuit of an Alberta franchise in high-decibel nationalism, convinced much of the province's business press to share his view. They all but anointed CanWest the licencee-apparent.

The company Asper had conceived while still leader of Manitoba's Liberals had grown astonishingly in twenty years. The greater part of that growth had been accomplished by using financial leverage to acquire existing businesses at a discount, and it had come at a considerable personal cost to the man from Minnedosa and his associates.

Gerald Schwartz, the brilliant young lawyer from Asper's pre-political days, had gone to New York and learned the predatory magic of leveraged buyouts, wherein the very success of an undervalued target corporation is used against it, its cash flow mortgaged to repay the debt incurred to scoop it up.

Schwartz returned to Winnipeg, and in 1977, he and Asper went into business together as self-described "merchant bankers," transforming CanWest Broadcasters into CanWest Capital Corporation. One of their first acquisitions was 60 per cent of Ontario's money-losing Global Television Network. (In fact, what they acquired was a Toronto licence granted in the "third-service" round in 1974, plus a number of rebroads that gave Global coverage over most of southern Ontario.) A few transactions later, Asper's CKND partners Seymour Epstein, who had acted as an engineering consultant to the Ontario undertaking, and Winnipeg movie-chain owner Paul Morton emerged with the other 40 per cent of Global. In 1979, CanWest extended a loan to another struggling station, CKVU-TV Vancouver. CanWest later added that station to its stable as well, after a five-year court battle with rival bidders. Outside of broadcasting, the Asper-Schwartz team acquired a hardware store chain, a fertilizer maker and a trust company, among other assets.

By the mid-eighties, however, the CanWest boardroom had become a danger-pay zone. Schwartz parted company with his former mentor in 1984, with considerable acrimony. Asper kept the pair's broadcasting assets; Schwartz took the rest (out of which he would create Onex Corporation, a financial empire that by 1999 was big enough to attempt a takeover of virtually the entire Canadian airline industry). Three years later Asper was in a legal brawl with his two remaining partners, Morton and Epstein, for control of Global. That dispute went through the courts too, before ending in late 1989 in a corporate shoot-out that pitted Asper against his ex-partners in an auction for each other's share of the Ontario TV service. Asper won, and CanWest went through another name change, becoming CanWest Global Communications Corporation.

By then, Asper had been introduced to a tactic even more bellicose—not to say bizarre—than a court action for resolving one's business disputes. In 1986, CanWest had applied to open a new television service—in Saskatchewan. It proposed new local stations in each of Saskatoon and Regina, finally bringing the province "third service." The province's existing broadcasters fiercely opposed any new licence being issued. They feared for their own survival in a market which at the time was literally shrinking: 5,000 people left Saskatchewan between 1986 and 1991, the province's population even dipping at one stage below the benchmark of one million. The CRTC, evidently skeptical, awarded CanWest a licence anyway. The Saskatchewan broadcasters then ventured on a manoeuvre that Asper would long remember. They went political.

Not just political: wide-open, full-throated *Political* at the highest level possible. Invoking a rarely used clause in the Broadcasting Act that permits the appeal of CRTC rulings to the federal Cabinet, the province's TV owners took their case to Conservative Prime Minister Brian Mulroney and his ministers. The politicians ordered the CRTC to reconsider the matter at new hearings, but the commission demonstrated its independence by confirming its original decision. CanWest's STV went on the air in 1987.

With the acquisition of CKVU-TV in Vancouver and a Maritime television chain earlier in the year, CanWest by 1993 had a presence in six provinces. With a net after-tax profit of $15 million on revenues of $235 million in its previous year, it was also Canada's richest private broadcaster. There were two secrets to its success. With its growing system of stations (and pockets that had deepened considerably during Schwartz's involvement with the company), CanWest could and did shop for the hottest of U.S. hits—the ten to fifteen top-rated dramas and sitcom series which, in any given season, perennially earned up to 80 per cent of most private TV station revenues in Canada. Over the years, in fact, CanWest Global had become an important supplier of those hit shows to other Canadian stations—buying national rights to series like *Melrose Place, Cheers, Frasier* and *Seinfeld,* then reselling regional or provincial rights to other broadcasters.

As it loaded up its schedule with audience-magnets made in America, CanWest Global was also in the happy position of being able to duck at least some of the requirements to support Canadian programming that drained cash from its competitors. Although its stations broadcast in more than half the provinces, in markets accounting for two-thirds of the Canadian audience, and its sales efforts energetically courted national advertising campaigns, CanWest was not licensed separately as a television *network* by the CRTC, as the CBC and CTV networks were. (This held until new regulations were issued in 1999; Global is now treated on the same basis as other networks.) As a result, while CanWest's local stations were required to contribute a percentage of their revenues or air time to Canadian television and film productions, the company as a whole escaped these additional expectations. With fewer obligations to Canadian content, and the cash to lock up the top U.S. shows, Global could hardly fail to outperform its rivals. With breathtaking audacity, the country's biggest exhibitor of American programming nonetheless based its case for an Alberta TV licence on an unabashed appeal to Canadian patriotism.

But there was one other player in the pack—a wild card by any definition. David Mackenzie was a thin, rumpled guy more comfortable in jeans and a bush shirt than in a three-piece pinstripe. The heir to a shipping fortune, Mackenzie had led a life that was colourful and eclectic.

In the 1980s, he had made a number of film documentaries—including *The Boys on the Bus*, about the Stanley Cup champion Edmonton Oilers. He was also a qualified helicopter pilot, and in the late eighties and early nineties had worked ferrying geologists from work-camp to work-camp around the Northwest Territories. As it happened, one geologist who hired Mackenzie was a canny fellow from Kelowna, British Columbia, named Charles Fipke, who was convinced there were diamonds in the Canadian Arctic. When the samples Fipke collected under Mackenzie's eye proved he was right, the helo pilot was among the first to invest in Fipke's Dia Met Minerals Ltd., at 17 cents a share. The value of those shares would climb to $60 each by the time Fipke's persistence was rewarded with the opening of Canada's first diamond mine in 1998.

By 1993, Mackenzie's holdings had already made him wealthy enough to go looking for something new and diverting to do with his time. In partnership with long-standing associate and fellow Dia Met investor Wayne Fipke (who, as well as being Charles Fipke's brother, had managed Edmonton's Citadel Theatre for a spell in the 1980s), Mackenzie began toying with the idea of taking a run at television.

If CanWest Global Communications Corp. were a buggy, it would be hitched to a high-stepping team of hackneys named Moxie and Chutzpah. Urged ever forward by a CEO who believes down to his follicles that two plus two can be made to equal six, "they really, really turn up the heat," observes Boyd Craig. "They play the political game very astutely, put out a lot of press releases, get on the cover of *Maclean's*. They convince people their way of seeing things is the natural way."

It certainly worked with the Alberta business press. Through the summer and fall of 1993, numerous reports uncritically carried Asper's boast that "Every time we open a station, we repatriate an audience that is watching U.S. channels." Few, if any, noted that the "repatriation" was accomplished by having the audiences watch the same U.S. sitcoms and series, only on Asper's channel.

Nor was there much media probing of the ebullient Asper or his designated Alberta lieutenant Don Brinton on the specifics of what their new station would truly bring to viewers. The tone of the pair's commitments was well captured in Asper's promise, oft-repeated with the adjectives in slightly different order, of an "independent, non-network, stand-alone, locally autonomous" TV outlet. Brinton added something less than clarity when he explained on another occasion that the service would be "alternative while remaining conventional."

Brinton managed more than once to make a meal of his own shoe leather. Programming on CanWest's proposed station, he acknowledged, would essentially replicate what was already running on Edmonton's CITV. In a further slight to that city's civic pride, Brinton let slip that most of the 100 jobs CanWest expected to create would be located in Calgary—Edmonton would get only a skeleton staff feeding material to the southern centre. Most startling of all, with the CRTC still months away from holding hearings into the licence applications—let alone making a decision to award a permit to anyone—Brinton told the media that CanWest's bid had already "gained acceptance" from the regulator.

The Craigs doubted that. They had too much experience with the commission to question its capacity to confound predictions. But as the deadline for finalizing the applications loomed at the end of September 1993, they had trouble on their hands.

The Craigs had relatively few worries about their program proposals. A-Channel, as Craig Broadcasting planned to brand the new service, would target the audiences Drew and Jodi—an active partner in planning the channel's program line-up—believed the existing broadcasters were missing. It would focus its identity on local news (with an emphasis on live coverage), children's programming and movies. The approach owed much to the experience at MTN, and it aimed to free the station from slavery to Hollywood series product.

Side-stepping interurban rivalry, they planned to create identically staffed production centres in Calgary and Edmonton—each with more jobs than the entire CanWest proposal. And twenty years after Stuart had offered to buy dozens of Kodak film cameras for community producers in Winnipeg, the Craigs held out to Alberta's growing film and TV production industry two commodities even more valuable in the nineties: money and air time. Craig Broadcast Systems committed to spend $16 million on independent Alberta productions over the anticipated seven-year term of a new licence, and to reserve space on its Sunday night prime-time schedule for airing the resulting product.

The commitment to local production was so large and unequivocal, in fact, that it reduced A-Channel's opponents to questioning whether the Craigs could afford it. The criticism struck home. Among themselves, the Craigs were confident their numbers would work. But their critics were right about one thing: Craig Broadcast had trouble on the financial side. And, for the first time since Stuart had taken control of Western Manitoba Broadcasters Ltd. two decades before, those troubles were threatening the corporate side as well.

The Craig application proposed that a new company called The Alberta Channel Inc., provisionally incorporated in August 1993, would own and operate A-Channel. Craig Broadcast Systems Inc. would hold 87 per cent of its shares. Initially, the plan was for a Lloydminster broadcaster, MidWest Television Ltd., to hold the other 13 per cent.

MidWest owned a twin-stick television operation in the Lloydminster market, which straddled the Alberta/Saskatchewan border, carrying CBC and CTV service to the area. Like Craig Broadcast Systems, MidWest was a family company. Its president, Mary Shortell, was the widow of its founder. MidWest's investment in the roughly $20 million it would take to launch new outlets in Edmonton and Calgary, though relatively small, was welcome. More so was the grounding in Alberta issues, personalities and business culture that a local partner could provide.

But Craig was not in a position to finance its own end entirely from internal sources. Through the late spring and early summer of 1993, the company had received several assurances from Roy Nat Inc., a Toronto corporate lender, that the finances it needed would be available when the filing deadline arrived. With that date only weeks away, Roy Nat backed out of the deal. Stu was livid. "We were double-crossed," he fumed. "They kept saying they'd lend us the money, and at the last minute they pulled the plug."

The Toronto lender's pullback was a shattering blow to the Craigs's hopes. "I remember sitting in a hotel room in Calgary thinking, 'This is it,'" Boyd recalls. (As it turned out, by the time the CRTC hearing was held in January 1994, the Craigs would obtain alternative bank financing. But in the fall of 1993, this had not yet been secured.)

Amid all the additional issues that have come to be addressed by the CRTC in the awarding of broadcast licences over the years, one question is unchanged: "Do you have the money?" The commission expects any applicant for a radio or television licence to supply it with both a signed commitment of what it describes as "unequivocally available funds" and the identity of those individuals or corporations providing them. The Craigs suddenly found themselves scrambling.

And now CanWest's hype campaign began to show its effect. "The sentiment at the time," says Boyd, "was, 'You guys don't have a hope in hell, why should we waste our time investing in your company?'"

The answer would come from an unexpected quarter. If most of the press had already written off the Craigs's chances, the odds being offered on the rest of the pack were even longer. Indeed, by then the field had been reduced to one: Wilks had finally recognized that his aspirations for ATN were going nowhere. Unable to scare up even a ghost of the necessary financing, Wilks sold his files and application documents to David Mackenzie and his partner, Wayne Fipke. Those two, through an entity called Alberta Interactive Multimedia Inc. (AIM), had filed a licence application with the CRTC, based heavily on Wilks's outlines, at the end of September. But with the CRTC's early December deadline for final applications fast approaching, the two entrepreneurs had growing misgivings about their chances.

Late in October, the phone rang in Stuart Craig's office. A mutual acquaintance wanted to know whether Craig would be interested in joining forces with Mackenzie and Fipke's bid. The caller had no way of knowing how welcome the inquiry was. "We had the application filed," recalls Stuart, "but as the deadline approached we were having trouble raising money. This guy had money big time."

In a flurry of correspondence, a basic understanding was quickly arrived at. In return for dropping the AIM bid and making an equity investment in the proposed new TV service, the owners of AIM would get 33 per cent of The Alberta Channel Inc. (One look at Wilks's warmed-over application convinced the Craigs it was worthless. Said Stuart: "We threw the whole thing away.") MidWest's interest in the proposed venture would drop to 10 per cent. With 57 per cent, the Craigs would keep control of the new company's operations. On October 28, the three parties signed a Memorandum of Understanding confirming the terms of the agreement—conditional upon the CRTC awarding A-Channel a licence. Seven days later, the document was filed with the CRTC, along with a statement disclosing the change in ownership and equity financing of the proposed service.

The Memorandum of Understanding was one degree short of the level of certainty that the Craigs's legal counsel, Toronto lawyer Peter Grant, would have liked to see. Grant, perhaps the most experienced communications law practitioner in the country, knew the CRTC might pounce on any imprecision or vagueness in a licencee's ownership. He urged the parties to execute the more formal Unanimous Shareholder Agreement, which had been filed in draft form. But Mackenzie, through his Edmonton lawyer Samy Salloum, seemed to be demanding a far greater role in the planned operation than the silent partnership the Craigs had cast him in. "They almost wanted to run the place," remembered Stuart. That was not about to happen. With the passing of the last deadline for locking in all application details, the clock ran out on negotiations.

Though they would not know it until much later, the failure to consummate the deal with AIM was one of the better breaks the Craigs had received in a while.

At hearings in January 1994, Craig Broadcast got another good break, of a somewhat elliptical sort. Having put themselves so unmistakably out in front in the media's perception of the licence competition, the CanWest proponents attracted the lion's share of the antagonism in the interventions filed by incumbent stations opposing both bids.

In the most extensive brief, WIC Western International Communications, the Vancouver-based owners of CITV and CITC, mocked A-Channel's commitment to live local news, quoting a study that described news programming from Craig Broadcast's Portage la Prairie station as "perfunctory, poorly written and uninspired." The same brief also challenged the Craigs's assertion that children's programs were wanting in the marketplace. But WIC found itself forced to pay the Brandon boys a compliment when it admitted that their commitments to local production were "a breath of fresh air."

WIC, backed by Electrohome and Baton, reserved most of its fire for the company that had declared the licensing process a foregone conclusion. In a heavily annotated analysis, WIC witheringly dissected CanWest's argument that it needed a presence in Alberta in order to bring viewers an extensive inventory—one company statement claimed as much as 5,210 hours—of high-quality Canadian programming not currently being shown in the province. By reviewing their own records of product purchased from Global over the years, Alberta's existing private broadcasters found that virtually every show Global's Toronto-based program division had pitched to them over the years had indeed been exhibited. The only exceptions were a few hours a week of Global news.

When, in the time leading up to the CRTC hearing, the incumbents pressed Global to itemize all those hours of Canadian programming that had gone unaired in Alberta, Global at first reduced its estimate (it explained that it had multiplied the actual available hours by four—because they might theoretically have been sold to all four existing private stations), then provided a list of programs that frankly astonished the Alberta broadcasters. None of them recognized a single title on the list. Pointedly, the WIC intervention noted:

> It also struck us that if there was all this product out there, why had Alberta broadcasters not been "pitched" on it? If the shows were of such high quality, it seems self-evident that not only would a serious sales attempt have been made, but the Alberta broadcasters would certainly remember screening the dubs of the shows in question which they apparently rejected. Unfortunately, that is not the case.
>
> The key point here, is that generally speaking, the programmers at the four Alberta stations have *absolutely no idea* [emphasis in original] what the remaining programs are!

The Albertans not only showed convincingly that there was no trove of unseen Canadian TV classics in Global's closet, they also catalogued Global's apparent lack of confidence in its own product list. While twenty-three of Global's portfolio of twenty-seven "foreign acquired"—a.k.a. U.S.—programs ran on at least three of its four stations, only two of its nine (verifiable) Canadian shows did. As the WIC brief laconically noted: "Very few CanWest Global Canadian shows enjoy the full system status that is the preserve of virtually every U.S. show which Global acquires."

As far as the incumbents could see, the likeliest result of licensing CanWest would be to deprive them of their highest-rated programming, which, they predicted, would be the only thing "repatriated"—to Global. "This movement of U.S. programming from the incumbent broadcasters to AltaWest [the CanWest subsidiary in whose name the licence was being sought] will leave the incumbents as the 'new' station in town, looking to replace the 70–80% of revenues generated by those top 10–15 programs," WIC concluded.

In the end, none of it would matter: neither Samy Salloum's ducking and weaving over the details of a Unanimous Shareholder Agreement, nor CanWest's mysterious arithmetic with programming. Apparently accepting another of the incumbents' arguments—that Alberta was no longer the gold mine it had been in the late eighties—the CRTC turned down both applications in June 1994.

Drew Craig, who for the first time had taken the point in stick-handling the A-Channel application through the hearing process, was devastated. "We were convinced, absolutely *convinced,* the commission was going to licence *somebody,*" he says. "It was quite a letdown. You'd almost feel better for somebody else to win."

Almost.

9

Off Camera

The bow came down in a long gliding stroke across the strings, and the dancers gave a small unconscious nod as they stepped out onto the floor. For the next few minutes, as long-legged cowpokes in their jeans and ladies in their petticoat skirts whirled and promenaded for the throng of eager fairgoers pressed against the rail, young Stuart Craig sweated and heaved to manhandle the heavy television camera on its wheeled dolly and keep the fast-moving square-dancers in its frame. Overhead, the concave dish antenna temporarily installed on the roof of this vast barn at the Manitoba Exhibition beamed the twirling images and the skirling reel of the fiddle over rooftops and back yards to a counterpart receiving antenna at the CKX studios, whence they were sent out across the prairie on the airwaves of Channel 5. It was the first television remote ever attempted in south-western Manitoba—and the implications were to stay in Craig's imagination for a very long time.

Over the years and decades that followed, Stuart Craig would dedicate himself to growing CKX's franchise and consolidating the family's control over the business. But he would never forget the potential of those microwaves. Indeed, even as he honed his skills at management, Stuart would periodically feel the tug of other ambitions. He was, by nature, a builder: the only other vocation he ever seriously considered was as an architect. And even though he would never take a formal course in engineering, he made it a point to understand not only the technology of the day in broadcasting, but the technologies of tomorrow. "I always admired his vision for the future," reflects Lawrence Dubois, who retired in 1996 as CKX's chief engineer. "He always knew where he was going."

Adds Bob Cornell, one of the *tres amigos* who dabbled in development in Brandon and Arizona with Craig: "He seemed to get his foot in the door first on a lot of things. He talked about digital television years ago; he saw it coming."

It is a passion that sets all of the Craigs apart from many self-styled broadcasters. "I insisted that my boys understand the technical side of the business," said Stuart Craig in later years. "For a broadcaster not to know how his plant runs is awful. If you don't understand how your system works, how are you going to know how to expand? How to make some money from it? I've talked to many television owners and managers, and as soon as we get into the technology, they have no idea." Stuart shook his head in disbelief. Of his own sons, he boasted: "We know the equipment, what you have to have. Engineers can't buffalo us."

On the contrary: in his restless attempts to expand his company's broadcast reach, Stuart Craig as often took the engineers aback. Especially on the subject of microwave, that band of high-energy, high-frequency electromagnetic radiation that was harnessed for cooking at just about the same time it was being put to work linking Canada's first transcontinental television network. As Stu learned more about microwave, he became ever more convinced that it could be made to bear enormous volumes of information—and that its cost could be brought down to a point that would prove it an economical vehicle for delivering programs directly to consumers' homes.

By the early eighties, Craig had developed a fully fledged business concept based on those insights. Essentially, his vision was for a cable-television distribution system ... without the cable. Microwaves were such workhorses they could be packed with literally dozens of discrete program channels, certainly at least as many as most cable carriers of the day offered. In Stu's vision, transmitters located on conventional broadcast towers would deliver their signals over a wide area within which consumers equipped with receiving antennas (far smaller than those required for signals from distant satellites) would be able to enjoy an entertainment menu at least the equal of what conventional coaxial cable provided. The system would have particular appeal in the many rural areas of the country where distance and low customer density made it uneconomic to install regular cable.

In 1983, Craig put his ideas on paper, along with the requisite folio of expert reports and studies affirming the soundness of his proposals, and submitted them to the federal Department of Communications. The government branch responsible at the time for approving the technical aspects of broadcasting sent his brief back to him without comment. Craig's ideas were so far ahead of anyone else's the department hadn't even begun to address the subject. (Later in the decade, Craig would submit his brief again. This time, much of the engineering model he employed would find its way into D.O.C.'s eventual regulatory framework for microwave program distribution.)

Stuart wouldn't give up his faith in microwaves, even when the disappointing responses from Ottawa began to mount up. "When we didn't get one licence," remembers Boyd, "it didn't seem a day would go by and he'd be working on another application." In fact, between 1983 and 1992, Craig submitted three further proposals to license microwave distribution in Manitoba. On each occasion, federal regulators (in the mid-eighties, the CRTC assumed responsibility for microwave proposals) turned him down.

In fairness, it was not really a case of obstinacy on the part of the commission. Its approach to new technologies has always been one of necessary caution. On the one hand, its mandate is to ensure that Canadians have orderly access to all the benefits of each new generation of communications technology. On the other, commissioners are obliged to be sensitive to the commercial reality of private companies who must, if they are to be viable, be permitted to amortize their investments in those self-same technologies over reasonable periods of time and a sufficient number of customers. The balancing act between those competing obligations constitutes much of the onus on commission panelists. It is their call to determine, in the case of broadcasting, when a market is rich enough to support additional competitors without cannibalizing existing radio or television stations. In a similar way, the commission for many years felt compelled to make fundamental choices among the new communication technologies competing for development during the 1970s and '80s, nurturing some with assigned protected markets, simply ignoring others.

Cable distribution of television programming, in that vision, was a favoured technology. Coax terminals soon joined electrical outlets and telephone wires as essential urban umbilica. And like the providers of those other services, cable television providers were given the advantage of monopoly rights to their markets.

There was a blank spot in the vision. It left in the dark millions of Canadians who lived in places where it was inconvenient or uneconomic to string cable, limiting them to two or at best three off-air channels while the rest of the world clicked its way toward a 50-going-on-500 channel universe. But those people were a minority. From the standpoint of the great majority of consumers, the CRTC seemed to have backed a winner.

In contrast to coax, commissioners for years dismissed microwave distribution as a "someday" technology: like direct-to-home satellite distribution, too expensive and too futuristic (and too likely to compete with the designated technology) to receive commercial approval.

By the 1990s, however, "someday" had come. Several factors pushed the CRTC to acknowledge a place for MDS, as it came be known (the acronym stood for *multipoint* distribution system, though, not microwave). One was the steady infiltration of rural Canada by "grey-market" satellite dishes whose owners subscribed to American program providers. Illegal, the practice was nonetheless politically and pragmatically beyond the reach of the CRTC to suppress.

Another factor was a sudden upsurge in the number of new technologies at least potentially subject to CRTC oversight: personal pagers, cellular phones, satellite phones, dedicated data cables and wireless links, fibre-optic trunk and distribution networks, pay- and pay-per-view TV. In the late eighties, four-fifths of the commission's time had been taken up by broadcasting issues. A decade later, the ratio had reversed: broadcasting occupied barely 20 per cent of the commission's energies as telecommunications issues mushroomed.

Increasingly, the CRTC backed away from micro-managing any of the technologies under its jurisdiction. In some cases, from managing at all. Faced with the new and unfathomable enormity of the Internet as the century closed, the CRTC in 1999 acknowledged its inability to enforce much of anything in cyberspace and formally withdrew from any regulation of the World Wide Web.

At the same time, the public's perception of economic efficiency was also shifting. Faith in market forces and confidence in the virtues of competition were replacing the traditional Canadian reliance on large, institutional agencies. Both the traditional phone companies and the long-standing cable monopolies had helped the process along with their lethargic indifference to consumers. The CRTC allowed the first tentative introduction of competition into the long-distance telephone business in the early nineties. Soon, in the arcane argot of commission cognoscenti, "convergence" became the buzzword. In 1995, the CRTC presented a policy statement on emerging technologies that came to be known as the "Convergence Report," although its formal title was "Competition and Culture on Canada's Information

Highway: Managing the Realities of Transition." "It was clear," the report observed, "that consumers desire more competitive distribution alternatives."

In August 1996, the Liberal federal government of Jean Chrétien agreed. Among other things, its formal policy statement envisioned the two great sets of connection networks that had evolved since the 1960s—the telephone companies ("telcos") and the cable companies—going head to head, after a suitable period of adjustment, in delivering services that up until then had been each one's monopoly preserve. That is, cable companies were to be allowed into the phone business, phone companies into the television distribution business: "convergence."

In light of those changing circumstances, the CRTC's views on MDS also evolved. In March of 1993, the commission held hearings in Ottawa to examine its policy on several emerging broadcast technologies—including satellite and terrestrial microwave distribution—and their potential impact on existing operators. Stuart Craig attended those hearings and presented a detailed brief urging the commission to accept MDS as a viable competitor to cable. As strongly, he argued that "wireless cable" licencees should be directed to put their first effort into serving rural areas the cable companies had hitherto ignored.

That June, the commission issued a new policy. There would be a place for MDS serving rural and remote customers—but not in competition with cable.

In the wake of disappointment in Alberta, the guiding minds at Craig Broadcast Systems might excusably have taken a breather. In Brandon and Portage la Prairie, a new generation of Craigs was bringing both joy and semi-permanent weariness to its parents. By the end of 1995, Drew and Jodi had three kids under the age of six at home. Boyd and Krista had as many.

Dillon, Drew and Jodi's son, was joined by a sister, Stephanie, in 1992, and another sister, Jamie, two years later. Boyd and Krista's Jonina was the first of four children to receive names in the tradition of their Icelandic forebears. She was followed by Freya in '92 and Gestny in '95. A son, Soren, came along in 1997.

When John Craig passed away peacefully on January 16, 1991, a month short of his ninetieth birthday, both of his granddaughters-in-law were pregnant: Jodi with Stephanie and Krista with Freya. Within the family, mourning for Johnny B.—Brandon's Mr. Hollywood, "the smartest man in the world," the visionary ex-goalie—was tempered by gratitude for the fullness of his life and the anticipated delight of two new arrivals.

For the first time, Shirley and Stuart had even taken a holiday. A *real* holiday, unconnected to an industry convention or a directors' meeting. In 1992, they drove down the spectacular cliff-hanging switchbacks of the northern California coastal highway, on the way to four weeks of leisure in Palm Springs. The two had a time they would treasure as a rare break from business. Even so, Stuart could not help noticing how the Palm Springs landscape and settlement patterns lent themselves to service by MDS.

Outside the family circle, business was going well. In Portage, MTN had settled into a steadily profitable groove—enhanced when the CRTC, in 1995, finally released it from the promise not to sell advertising to retail clients in Winnipeg. CKX-TV, though no gold mine, nonetheless continued to make its regular contribution to Craig Broadcast's bottom line.

The happy surprise of the decade had turned out to be radio. The medium that had started it all was once again going through a transformation, although this one would not be so evident to the listener. With the advent of computers, "live" disc-jockey patter could become one more prerecorded packet to be dropped into sequence between digitized tunes and agency commercials. Hosts could record enough "spontaneous" chat for a three-hour air shift in thirty minutes, then be on to other assignments—or off the clock. Except for high-value "drive" periods (so-called because they coincide with the morning and afternoon periods when rush-hour drivers are locked in their cars, a captive audience), it was practical to let automated stations run almost unattended. There were adjustment pains—including lost jobs—for stations that embraced the changing times and technology. But as the economies took hold, balance sheets at Canadian private radio stations began to look rosier than they had in more than decade.

Boyd Craig took it upon himself to turn the company's stumbling radio operations into a profit point. He was confident that the lessons of CKX could be applied pretty much anywhere, certainly in the Canadian West. With Stuart's approval, he began shopping. His first acquisition was a station called CFQX-FM. Located in Selkirk, thirty-five kilometres northeast of Winnipeg, the station, like CHMI-TV in

Portage la Prairie, was also received in the capital. Despite that advantage, CFQX had lost money for three years running. Late in 1993, the CRTC approved its sale to Craig for $1.65 million (a figure, Boyd notes, that included $400,000 in realizable tax losses). The station was transferred to its new owners on New Year's Day, 1994. "January is a terrible month for radio. I had told the bank we were going to lose money," Boyd says. But in the event, he recalls with satisfaction, "We *made* money."

After owning CFQX for less than a year, Craig did another radio deal that would release the station—for a while—from the family's string. In November 1994, Boyd reached an agreement with Clint Forster, a retired Saskatchewan cable entrepreneur who had sold his company in the early nineties and retired to Victoria to dabble in radio. The deal covered four stations and would cost Craig Broadcasting nearly $4 million by the time the offsets were all accounted for. At the end of the day, Forster's Western World Communications Ltd. got CFQX; Craig got a station in Winnipeg, CKMM-FM, as well as CIRK-FM, Edmonton and CKIT-FM, Regina. Disclosure documents indicated that the Selkirk and Regina stations had been losing money for at least three years.

The CRTC approved the transfers in August 1995, and Boyd soon discovered that the Edmonton station was losing money as well. Within eight months he had added a second outlet to Regina's CKIT and two years later sold CIRK, Edmonton, to Newfoundlander Harry Steele.

By the time the nineties faded out, CFQX would also be back in Craig hands, thanks to a pair of CRTC rulings. One for the first time permitted proprietors to own *two* AM and FM stations in markets served by eight or more local radio signals. The other decided that Selkirk was, for the purposes of relaxing the ownership limit, part of the Winnipeg market. It brought to six the number of stations owned by the Craigs. All were making money.

In early 1995, however, that turnaround was still over the horizon. One day in the spring of that year, as Boyd sat at his desk in Brandon glumly examining the financial reports of the three stations he had recently agreed to purchase, his father stuck his head inside the door.

"The call's out!" Stuart announced. "I'm going to apply for MDS."

"You're crazy!" his son shot back.

Crazy, maybe. Determined certainly. The application filed that

August in the name of Craig subsidiary SkyCable Inc. was Stuart's fourth attempt to win the CRTC's green light for a wireless cable system to serve rural Manitobans. It would be his most detailed and technically advanced proposal yet. And, at $26 million in anticipated commitment, his most expensive.

It would, in fact, be world-leading. In the previous few years, the federal Department of Communications had somewhat limited the potential for microwave distribution by reassigning some portions of the radio spectrum previously allocated to MDS to other uses, reducing the bandwidth available for commercial development. Offsetting this, however, were developments in video compression that permitted much more information to be packed into even that reduced bandwidth. Now, working with a Manitoba microengineering startup named Broadband Networks Inc., Craig proposed to go to the next technology plateau—delivering a digital signal.

For 50,000 rural Manitobans, many of whom now received only one or two off-air signals and some of whom were fifty kilometres from the nearest video store, MDS would mean interference-free, CD-quality video and audio on at least forty channels to begin with, and many more later. The nature of microwaves and Broadband Networks' technology, moreover, meant that SkyCable could deliver pay-TV and pay-per-view TV at an advantage over conventional cable, in that it did not require a separate set-top box. There was a further advantage over cable as well: unlike coax, SkyCable's receivers were individually addressable, meaning customers could select individual channels from a menu, a clear improvement on the predetermined packages of channels the cable industry obliged its customers to accept. With nine broadcast towers, the system, if approved, would deliver its clear signal to every home in Manitoba below the fifty-second parallel—making it not only Canada's first digital MDS system but the largest such system anywhere in the world.

"As a rural broadcaster of some 45 years," the application reminded the CRTC, "Craig would find it very satisfying, to say the least, to finally be in a position to bring multiple television programming options to its rural viewers, reducing the disparity that has existed for too long between rural and urban television viewers." But years of experience had also taught the family that the mere promise of bringing multiple-choice television to 50,000 new households would not likely be good enough to secure the CRTC's approval. The application also committed to public benefits worth an additional $3 million, mainly in cash contributed via granting agencies directly to Canadian (and specifically Manitoban) television and film production.

In many ways, it was a classic Craig application. Stu and the boys had no doubt that somewhere down the road the system they proposed would find its audience and turn into a profitable franchise. Meanwhile, there would be too much serious building to do to waste time counting beans. Going digital from the outset would raise the bar higher than it needed to be, but that was no different from housing TV and radio under one roof back in the fifties. And if the plan was financially risky and technically ground-breaking, it was also predicated on a thrifty use of existing assets: five of nine microwave transmitters proposed in the application would mount on existing Craig towers, substantially reducing capital outlay. The proposed benefits were neither inflated nor befogged in diversionary flim-flam.

Whatever its merits, the Craig application would not be unopposed. Winnipeg Videon Inc., the cable arm of Moffat Communications, together with a group of other cable companies including Calgary giant Shaw Cablesystems and tiny Westman Media Cooperative Ltd., a long-standing Brandon rival, had assembled a competing bid. And it soon became evident that the group had a silent but potentially powerful partner.

"The danger with a broadcast licence," acknowledges Boyd Craig, "is there always seems to be some political intrigue going on." In September of 1995, the intrigue became more than suspicion. Directed by the CRTC, the Videon group disclosed an agreement concluded *more than a year earlier* with the government of Manitoba. In opaque legalese, the document committed the cable companies to submitting an MDS application within 180 days and, once having received the CRTC's approval (which was apparently assumed), to completing construction of a system within three years. If they failed to do so, they were liable for a penalty of up to $3.5 million—the full amount of their proposed investment in MDS—to the province. In return, the province committed to consummate a separate deal between the Manitoba Telephone System (a provincial Crown utility at the time) and the cablers, in which the latter were assured of "the acquisition of certain assets." The assets in question? Hundreds of miles of extremely valuable installed coaxial and fibre-optic cable belonging to MTS, which the company had previously leased to the private cable carriers. They would henceforth own it.

It was an odd duck of a deal, to put it mildly. In exchange for the cable partners' undertaking to spend $3.5 million and "consider" the use of Manitoba suppliers, Tory Premier Gary Filmon had allied his government with a Calgary company against an all-Manitoba group committed to spending six times as much money and to showcasing the province's technology. "Clearly," Boyd Craig observes drily, "the government had an agenda."

The Craigs did what they could. "We went in to see the premier, asked him to reconsider," Boyd says. "They watered down their support, but it was still on the record."

On October 29, the CRTC made a crucial concession. In a policy amendment statement, the commission declared that it would not stand in the way of MDS providers who sought to woo away cable subscribers. Wireless cable, in short, had clearance to compete head to head with established cable networks. The next day, hearings on the Craig application and others began in Hull, Quebec.

The verdict arrived five days before Christmas, 1995. In dry bureaucratic language, CRTC Decision 95-910 stated: "Applications by SkyCable Inc. for new MDS radiocommunication distribution undertakings—approved; two competing applications—denied." It was a Christmas present Stuart Craig had been waiting for for a quarter of a century.

10

Big Game

In early February of 1996, the CRTC once again called for proposals for new television stations in Alberta.

It was less than six weeks since the commission had approved Stuart's long-held dream of building a microwave-based TV distribution system across all of southern Manitoba. The small suite of executive offices along the front of the CKX studio building in Brandon was hip-deep in engineers' drawings, coverage maps and marketing plans. But there wasn't much doubt about Craig Broadcast's response to the call. The decision to try again for the golden foothills hardly needed to be spoken aloud, let alone debated.

The Alberta market had only gotten richer, and its incumbent broadcasters fatter, in the three years since the last application call. Former Calgary mayor Ralph Klein was in the premier's office in Edmonton now, slashing provincial taxes. A growing number of corporate headquarters were pulling up eastern stakes and relocating to Klein's old hometown. The province's population had grown by 50 per cent in the twenty-three years since the last new television station had been licensed in Alberta. Complaints from advertisers about the sellers' market for air time were, if anything, even more bitter than at the beginning of the decade. Taking a second run at those licences was a no-brainer.

Then, in late March, the CRTC issued another call: for a TV licence in Vancouver. Calgary and Edmonton were by now the country's fifth- and sixth-largest markets. Along with the smaller centres of Red Deer and Lethbridge (and a trickle of program sales), the two cities were generating revenues of about $200 million a year for Alberta's private television broadcasters. Vancouver was the country's No. 3 market overall, its second-biggest English market. It did $200 million a year all by itself. And viewers there hadn't had a new local television station in two decades either. The Craigs began to give *that* some thought.

At CanWest Global, Izzy Asper was increasingly turning decisions

Right: Radio "remotes" went mobile in the 1960s, when CKX acquired a studio-in-a-trailer.

Below: Portable sound recording was bulky, but sturdy enough to withstand barnyard use!

CKX - TV COLOR
RCA
RCA TP66

Above: By 1967, Canada's centennial year, John Craig had withdrawn from day-to-day management of the company he began. Within a year, Stuart Craig would become managing director at age thirty-four.

Facing page: A new telecine machine, acquired in 1969, brought colour television to screens in southwest Manitoba. But viewers grumbled that CKX was keeping the new CTV service out of the region.

Above and left: A second CKX tower, 412 metres tall, collapsed in 1983, when several days of freezing rain left heavy coatings of ice on its metalwork and guy wires. Luckily, this time no one was hurt.

Left: Stuart and Shirley Craig visited Las Vegas in the early seventies on a rare holiday. Stuart called his wife his most important business advisor, "my partner in everything."

Below: Twenty years of research and persistence paid off in late 1995, when the CRTC approved Craig Broadcast System's proposal for wireless cable. Shown here, *left to right,* are Miles, Stuart, Drew and Boyd Craig.

Facing page: Drew and Jodi Craig are shown here celebrating the opening of A-Channel's new Calgary headquarters in September 1997. Within two years, the Craig station would lead in the local market's prime-time ratings.

Above: Downtown locations, live local morning shows and a fleet of bright yellow "Hummvee" four-wheel-drive vehicles stamp the new A-Channel's identity on the public mind in both Calgary *(pictured)* and Edmonton.
Keith Levit photo

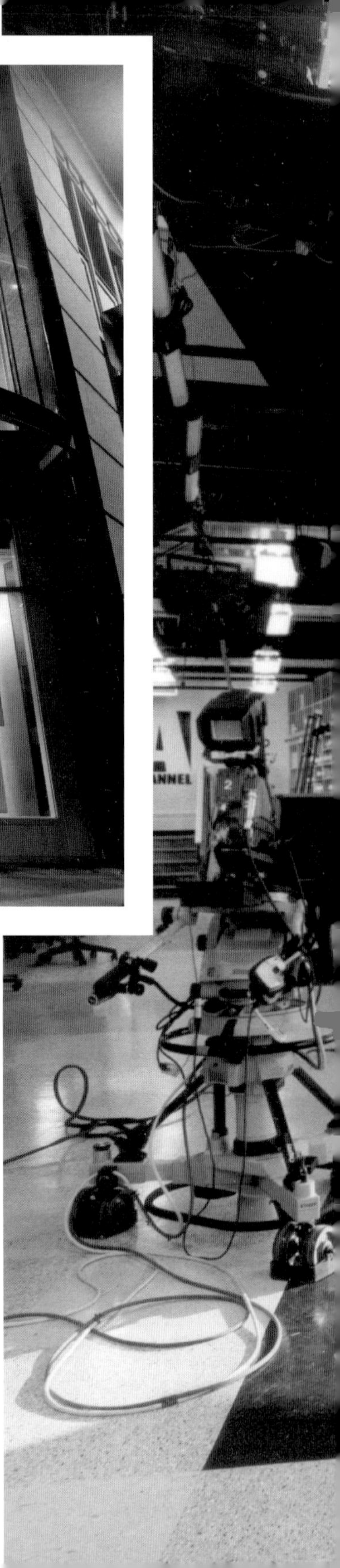

Right: Work space for journalists, producers' desks and dozens of television screens do double duty as backdrops when broadcasts go live-to-air several times daily from A-Channel's all-digital studios.
Keith Levit photo

News
CHANNEL

Stuart Craig, pictured at the September 1999 opening of A-Channel Manitoba's new studios at The Forks in Winnipeg, died a month later, on October 30, 1999. "One of the good ones is gone," lamented fellow broadcaster Ken Clark.

over to his sons, Leonard and David, and his daughter, Gail. But the company's appetites were unabated. A competing CanWest application for Alberta was a given.

But in other respects the field in all three cities—and, for that matter, across Canada—had changed greatly in the short time since the Craigs had made their last Alberta application. One former national broadcasting powerhouse had vanished entirely. A second was in the process of withdrawing from play. Yet a third was imploding on a failed generational transition. A fourth was showing unexpected vigour in a daring strategy to unify a fractured national network.

All but the last had once been forces to reckon with in Alberta. As the years and deals had reshuffled the deck, however, a worrying trend had emerged. Between 1989 and 1996, Alberta had gone from having four distinct independent private television operators in its two main cities, to three. Absent a new entrant, within a year the number might be down to two.

The consolidation had begun in 1989, when Vancouver-based WIC Western International Communications acquired CFAC-TV Calgary (later renamed CICT-TV) from Maclean Hunter Ltd., following its acquisition of Selkirk Communications Inc. that year. Within a year, WIC had multiplied the Calgary station's value by acquiring Edmonton's CITV from Griffiths's contemporary and friend, Dr. Charles Allard, together with Allarcom's interests in specialty and pay-TV. That reduced the number of independent private television broadcasters in Alberta to three and made WIC the first private owner to achieve coverage in both its major cities. It was WIC—with its two non-network-affiliated stations—that had put up the most spirited defence of Alberta's rich turf back in 1993.

At the time, the owners of the province's two CTV outlets had largely ridden along on WIC's intervention.

CFCN-TV Calgary's corporate parent at the start of the decade was Maclean Hunter Ltd. Maclean Hunter was a large, rich and profitable company with one fatal weakness: a widely held stock. By 1993, its management was deeply preoccupied with fighting off unwanted takeover attempts. Within a year, the company would surrender to Rogers Communications Inc., the cable giant.

The other CTV station in Alberta in 1993, CFRN Edmonton, was owned by Electrohome Limited. That company had once manufactured home stereos and continued to make a range of visual communication hardware for business. Its management wanted to refocus on those manufacturing roots. By the middle of the decade, Electrohome's radio and television stations were considered peripheral assets soon to be on the block.

WIC would of course intervene once again, to object that it and Alberta's two other private television broadcasters could not afford additional competition. Its intervention would also provide a trenchant analysis of the marked differences between the Craig and the CanWest visions of expansion into Alberta. But at WIC's head office, minds were on other things.

On April 7, 1994, WIC founder Frank Griffiths had died. In sharp contrast to the Craigs (and, it must be said, to the Aspers), the Griffiths would offer a textbook example of how *not* to pass on the family company torch. At the time of the senior Griffiths's death, his eldest son, Frank Jr., was WIC deputy chairman. The family's control of WIC was absolute, exercised through its ownership of all but a handful of WIC's voting A shares.

The great majority of shareholder equity in the company was held by the public and a few other large investors—including the Allard Family's Cathton Holdings Ltd. and CanWest. But the equity resided in the form of non-voting B shares. Under certain circumstances, and specifically if control of the company ever changed hands, those B shares were supposed to convert to voting A's, a "coat-tail" arrangement that had the potential to trigger an earthquake under WIC's management. While the Griffiths family kept its voting share block, however, its control could not be challenged.

At Frank Sr.'s death, his shares in WIC went to his widow, Emily. The mantle of the media giant's $250-million-a-year business should have fallen on Frank Jr.'s shoulders. But it didn't. Frank's management style, as his sister Mary once described it to the *Financial Post,* was prone to "interference, throwing his weight around, second-guessing [and] bad-mouthing." Almost immediately the Allard family, who had inherited Dr. Charles's interest in WIC on his death, revolted. After some tense meetings, the Allards agreed to swallow their unhappiness with the new generation of Griffiths leadership in return for a boost in their holding in WIC voting stock and the installation of one of their own as co-chairman with Frank Jr. Emily Griffiths kept 61 per cent of the all-important A shares, a position that retained at least the façade of family control and, just as importantly, avoided triggering the coat-tail provision. Within ten months, WIC's two co-chairmen resigned. Young Frank was demoted to vice-president.

Frank Sr. had built well. WIC's businesses continued to thrive. The company was the country's highest-billing station group, with nine TV licences, including CHCH-TV Hamilton and CFCF-TV in Montreal (the direct descendent of Marconi's pioneering station), a dozen radio stations, interests in pay- and satellite TV, and revenues of close to half a billion dollars a year. It had extremely capable professional managers. But absent a controlling shareholder to give them strategic direction, the company was adrift. In September 1996, with Emily Griffiths's consent, Frank Jr. was removed as WIC vice-president and left the company.

As it happened, younger son Arthur had lost the rest of the family's heritage that same summer, when he was forced to relinquish control of the Vancouver Canucks NHL team, and the lavish new arena he had built for them, to the McCaw family of Seattle.

Then again, there still *was* a WIC head office. Maclean Hunter, as a broadcaster, had simply vanished after Rogers's $3.1-billion takeover. (A rump entity named Maclean Hunter Canadian Publishing Ltd. continued turning out *Maclean's* and some other print titles for a few years, before being absorbed into Rogers Media.) With the 1994 takeover, however, the cable giant had incurred a $2 billion debt. It had also been required, as a condition of the takeover, to sell CFCN-TV Calgary and its interest in CTV to a third party. In June 1996, just days before the start of hearings into the new Alberta licence applications, the CRTC approved the transfer of CFCN-TV to Baton Broadcasting.

The deal brought something to Baton that it considered of even greater value than a television station in Calgary. Along with the CFCN-TV licence went a one-seventh share in CTV, the network cooperative launched in the mid-sixties. CFCN had been one of the original "seven sisters," stations that had signed on in Vancouver, Calgary, Edmonton, Toronto, Montreal and Halifax, at the same time as the Moffats' CJAY (later CKY) had in Winnipeg. As a cooperative, the network had always suffered from underfunding and the divided priorities of its proprietors. Now, a new force at work inside Baton—the licencee of CFTO-TV Toronto, one of the original seven and regarded as CTV's flagship—was determined to change that.

His name was Ivan Fecan, and in February 1996, he was forty-two. A baby-faced, silver-haired wunderkind of the Toronto broadcast scene, Fecan had made his first mark creating CityPulse News for CHUM's hip CITY-TV in the late seventies. The CBC had wooed Fecan (pronounced "Fet-*san*"; the Ivan as "I-*vahn*") away from CITY in 1980, and after senior assignments at the public network and at NBC in New York, he had joined Baton as a senior group vice-president in 1994. Within months he was executive vice-president and chief operating officer. By 1997, he would be president. And, with the backing of the company's principal shareholders—the Eaton and Bassett families—he was a man with a plan.

The acquisition of CFCN-TV in Calgary gave Baton two of CTV's seven votes. At the same time, Fecan had done a parallel agreement with Electrohome, owner of CFRN-TV Edmonton (another of the seven sisters), as well as of CKCO-TV in Kitchener. That agreement—which also required CRTC approval, received in mid-1996—pooled Baton and Electrohome's stations in Alberta and Ontario in new holding companies in which the two were equal partners. Meanwhile, Electrohome undertook to vote CFRN's CTV network share with Baton. That gave Fecan three of seven CTV votes.

The back-to-back deals with Rogers and Electrohome effectively did two other things. They gave Baton/Electrohome a presence in both of Alberta's major markets. And they reduced the number of private television providers in those markets to within a technicality of two. Even that technicality would evaporate the following year, when Baton acquired Electrohome's station and its CTV share outright. Henceforth, the Alberta market would be regarded as a two-station play—with outlets in both Calgary and Edmonton—or nothing.

Once again, CanWest entered the lists wearing the assumption of victory like a cockade. Compared to Craig Broadcast Systems, CanWest was a Goliath: big, brazen and *rich*. Its revenues that year were running at $370 million, not quite up to the level of WIC's $457 million, but ahead of Baton's $225 million. More telling was the wide difference in what each of the three giants of English-language Canadian broadcasting was making in profits on those revenues. At 16 per cent, Baton's cash flow margin was the lowest of the three; its gross earnings that year would be only about $36 million. WIC was doing better, retaining 22 per cent of its revenues—about $100 million in 1996. But CanWest was just burning down the barn, with margins running at 35 per cent. In 1996, CanWest's earnings before interest, depreciation and taxes would be more than $125 million. It was the most profitable broadcaster in Canada.

As big and rich as it was, CanWest wanted to be even more so. Indeed, that was the very essence of the Asper group's case: that in order to fund quality Canadian television programs, CanWest needed to be wealthy and powerful enough to compete on an equal footing with U.S. media giants for national rights to *American* shows (the enormous profits from which, the argument ran, would then support Canadian production). To get to the requisite size, CanWest argued, it needed to have a full national network. To that end, the company had other applications before the CRTC at the same time: first, to acquire an existing CBC-affiliated station in Quebec City, converting it to a Global affiliate and adding transmitters in Montreal and Sherbrooke, and second, to add a station in Victoria.

There were two odd aspects to this line of appeal by CanWest. The first was that the company was already perfectly able to buy Canadian rights for U.S. programming, as well as to amortize that cost across audiences in every region. Indeed, its Global subsidiary was the country's largest distributor of American-made shows to regional independent stations—like the incumbents in Calgary and Edmonton. Moreover, if CanWest was correct that size translates into support for Canadian production, it was curious that the dynamic had yet to manifest itself in CanWest's own buying patterns. As the CRTC was aware, the richest Canadian broadcasting company in fact spent less of its revenue on homegrown production (18 per cent) than practically anyone else in the country. CTV, by contrast, spent one-third of its income on Canadian shows.

Craig Broadcast's vision of an "innovative, interactive and independent alternative" Alberta service named A-Channel could not have been more different. Where CanWest argued that its own expansion was synonymous with public benefit, the Craig application contained precise and specific commitments to Alberta. The most significant was an entirely new, multimillion-dollar fund to support the homegrown movie and TV productions for which money had always been hardest to raise: long-form drama. Where CanWest argued that Canadian content was only possible if CanWest was able to exhibit American shows coast to coast, Craig proposed a completely revolutionary program concept. Canadian- and Alberta-made shows, far from being a peripheral good deed relegated to the margins of prime-time Americana, were going to be at the heart of A-Channel's broadcast schedule.

The years since the last Alberta round had also brought the Craigs new and persuasive allies. Drew Craig had not stopped wooing Alberta film and television producers after the CRTC's rejection of the company's 1993 licence bid. Quite the opposite. The courtship paid off handsomely when Drew asked Joanne Levy, a respected and well-connected Alberta current affairs and educational TV producer, to help sell the CRTC on the Craig application. "The biggest problem [facing A-Channel] was one I had to deal with myself," she acknowledges. "It was, 'Oh yeah, sure!'"

"As an independent producer in Alberta," says Levy, "I'd seen an awful lot of promises from a lot of people. I was very, very cynical about any broadcaster who came bearing gifts." But as she checked out the Craigs with her network of contacts in television, Levy says, "I was quite taken by their vision and their integrity. If they say they're going to do something, they do it." Levy was even more taken by Craig Broadcast's commitment to spend $14 million on made-in-Alberta movies and television production. "That was something that was different, that was unique. No one had really come to the table with so much enthusiasm before." Levy agreed to sign on to represent the A-Channel Drama Fund.

Another powerful presence on the Craig bench had arrived there by a more accidental route, although she herself would likely say it was no accident at all.

In the spring of 1990, Lisa Meeches had been fresh out of journalism school at the University of North Dakota in Minot, back home on her Ojibway Nation reserve near Portage la Prairie, and unemployed. One Monday morning the phone rang. A male voice on the other end identified himself as Boyd Craig, with local television station MTN. Craig offered her a job. "I said, 'Get lost!' and hung up on him," Meeches remembers with a laugh. "I'm thinking, no one's going to phone a little Indian girl with no industry experience and say they're going to hire you! I thought it was one of my brothers."

Happily, Boyd phoned back. "That Tuesday, I was reporting news," Meeches recalls. After nine months on general assignment, she was asked to report on aboriginal affairs—from a native standpoint and with a positive take on stories. Articulate, intelligent, poised and attractive, the "little Indian girl" (who at the age of four had confided to her grandfather her ambition to be on television one day), was soon hosting a weekly half-hour native-affairs newsmagazine called *The Sharing Circle*. Craig Broadcasting gave her a budget that enabled her to assemble a board of "spiritual advisors" and to "feast" the show at the start of each season in a gesture of respect for the spirits of the stories that would be told in the episodes ahead.

In the year before the Alberta application, the Craigs had done something even more remarkable. "The boys," as Meeches calls them, "said to me, 'We're the only ones benefiting from your show. We want you to benefit. We'll sell you the show and buy back the rights.'" Such an arrangement would give Meeches not only a significant slice of advertising revenue from the show (from the sale of avails not included in the rights purchase), but equity in the program's growing library and the opportunity to profit from its resale. "They sold me the show for $10—which I still owe them!" Now, in 1996, Meeches was a passionate and disarming exponent of A-Channel's eagerness to reflect Alberta's aboriginal people in new local versions of the successful *Sharing Circle* format.

The Craigs's reputation for standing by their commitments had shown a return on the financial side of the application as well. This time, there would be no need for last-minute scrambling for loans or demeaning meetings in which their chances against the CanWest juggernaut were dismissed. For the first time, an institutional investor was wholly committed to a Craig undertaking: TD Capital Group was prepared to put up cash to hold 29.9 per cent of the proposed operating company, A-Channel Inc. MidWest Television, the Craigs's initial junior partner in the 1993 application, was back in 1996 with 10.5 per cent.

If Craig Broadcast decided to go after the Vancouver call, the forces at work would be different again—although many of the same players were in the game. The fight, for starters, was for one market instead of two. And the second-largest English-speaking market in the country at that.

British Columbia had roughly 4 million people. Two-thirds of them—equivalent to Alberta's entire population—clustered in the lower mainland around Vancouver, the province's largest city, and in the bottom end of Vancouver Island around the capital, Victoria. Most of those nearly 3 million people were within the coverage areas of all four local Canadian stations and one just over the border, in Bellingham, Washington. KVOS, the U.S. station, was estimated to be draining at least $25 million of advertising revenue a year from the Vancouver/Victoria market. The CBC had a station and production centre in Vancouver and actively sold local advertising there. CanWest also had a presence, in CKVU-TV.

The 900-pound gorilla in the market was WIC. Despite the unmistakable *fin de régime* air around its downtown Vancouver executive suite, WIC ruled its home turf. It owned two of the three private stations serving the region. In Vancouver, CHAN-TV (better known to viewers as BCTV) was the local CTV affiliate; as one of the original seven sisters, it also held a voting share in the network. Through rebroads, BCTV was seen virtually throughout British Columbia. As well, WIC had the licence for CHEK-TV in Victoria. This apparent departure from the CRTC policy against common ownership of duplicate licences in the same market was explained by the argument that Victoria and Vancouver were, in fact, distinct markets, much like Portage and Winnipeg. In its own notices, however, the commission frequently treated the two as one.

Already the overwhelmingly dominant local player, WIC would be the only major Canadian broadcasting company to sit out the Vancouver licence call.

Remarkably, CanWest, the only other private station owner in urban British Columbia, had applied to become the new licensee as well. In a bid to reach parity with WIC, CanWest sought a licence in Victoria to pair with its existing Vancouver outlet.

Baton, with Fecan at the whiphand of an expansion drive, also applied. Winning a licence for its proposed independent outlet, however, would put Baton in the peculiar position of owning a station opposing the CTV affiliate in the market (WIC's CHAN/BCTV), even as Fecan bore down on control of the private network.

Rogers Broadcasting was also at the gate. Despite dealing CFCN Calgary to Baton earlier in the year, the company controlled by unpredictable Toronto cable and cel-phone king Ted Rogers was still, in a small way, in broadcast television. Its CFMT-TV in Toronto followed a unique multilingual, multicultural format. Rogers believed the formula would have appeal as well in Vancouver, whose residents were every bit as varied an ethnic mix as Toronto's.

The wild card in the pack was CHUM Ltd., proprietor of Toronto's cheeky CITY-TV. Best known for that urban-format station—whose signal was carried on numerous cable systems across the country—and its once-dominant Toronto rock radio station, CHUM also had a potpourri of other broadcasting assets. It owned CJCH-TV Halifax (a CTV affiliate and another of the network's seven share-holding "sisters") as part of a Maritime TV chain, as well as CKVR Barrie, in

CITY's Ontario back yard. Three of the country's most successful specialty cable channels also belonged to CHUM: Bravo!, MuchMusic and Space—The Imagination Station. Its revenues, at $240 million that year, rivalled those of Baton and CanWest. Vancouver would give it, for the first time, a direct-broadcast reach from coast to coast.

Leading the CHUM application was CITY's president, Moses Znaimer. Thin to the point of gauntness, with the look of a more intense Bill Murray, Znaimer had a gift for the Zen sound-bite and a Svengali-like attraction for the Vancouver punditti. Local TV critics would spend much of 1996 lionizing Moses's vision while, it was widely suspected, slipping him resumés.

Going for the Vancouver licence, in short, would put John Craig's grandkids from Brandon, Manitoba, into the ring against the four biggest English-language private broadcasters in the country. The smallest of them was ten times the size of Craig Broadcast Systems. Stuart, Drew, Boyd and Miles figured the competition was about even.

In early May, Drew and Boyd were in Vancouver preparing the ground for an application when they received a telephone call. It was their father. "You'd better come home," Stu told them.

Shirley Craig, the always quiet, always calm and supportive, always kind girl from across 22nd Street, the woman who had always shied away from doctors, had been diagnosed with cancer. On May 10, she died. "It was almost surreal, she went so fast," reflects Drew. "We all just didn't go into work for about ten days. We couldn't."

Stuart, recently given a clean bill of health after a brush with prostate cancer, lost the most important person in his life just three weeks short of their forty-eighth wedding anniversary. As his mother had done twenty-seven years earlier, his wife passed on so quickly it seemed almost inconceivable. "Both deaths were so sudden," notes his sister, Catherine Moffat. "That's why there was such a parallel when Shirley died. From the time she saw the doctor to the time she passed away was three weeks."

It was "one of the most difficult times for us as a company," Drew says. "My mother was a tremendous support to my dad. He never got over it."

But the clock was still ticking on the Vancouver call. It would not pause to accommodate the grief being felt in the Craig homes in Brandon and Portage la Prairie. A week after Shirley's death, the boys and Stuart finally forced themselves to address the subject. The deadline for applications was the end of the month. Feelings were mixed. The drive to launch SkyCable by autumn was soaking up both money and energy. Hearings on the Alberta licences loomed in July.

"Then," remembers Drew, "we thought, *she* would have wanted us to file the damn thing."

In a burst of energy that culminated in all-nighters in Portage la Prairie and a Hollywood hotel (where Drew and Jodi were scrambling to purchase programming for MTN's fall schedule, after missing the spring screenings for Shirley's funeral), Craig Broadcasting submitted its proposal to the CRTC.

It asked for a licence to establish VITV—Vancouver Independent Television—in Vancouver.

11

A Tale of Two Cities

Canmore is a linear town, strung out along the length of the Trans-Canada Highway and the railway that runs alongside it. Both, like the town itself, are squeezed into a fold of the Rocky Mountains between Calgary and Banff. In the side valleys to north and south are miles of trails where cross-country skiers in winter and hikers in summer breathe pure air and soak up the humbling beauty of peaks that reach to heaven between green forested slopes. Downtown, just across a rushing, glacier-fed stream from the endless river of traffic on the highway, are a score or so of local service businesses and an equal number of restaurants and bars aimed at the travellers and tourists who are Canmore's economic lifeblood. In 1988, this was the site of the cross-country skiing and biathlon events of the winter Olympics. In 1996, it was where the A-Channel team came to prepare for the CRTC's hearing into competing applications for the new television licences in Alberta.

For the participants, the two events had much in common. "You don't sleep much the night before," Drew Craig admits. "You've got a lot riding on it. You take nothing for granted. All you can do is do the best you can."

Like politicians preparing for a televised debate, the rival camps in a significant CRTC hearing spend the final few days before their events honing their focus, trying to anticipate every contingency. For Craig Broadcast, preparations on the eve of battle included tweaking the text they would present during arguments in-chief, rehearsing the order in which the team would speak, and submitting to volleys of questions on every possible facet of the application which anyone, panellist or intervenor, might raise at the hearing. Firing the questions in the living room of the hotel suite the company had rented in Canmore was an affable, silver-haired Toronto lawyer named Peter Grant. A senior partner at McCarthy Tétrault, the country's largest law firm, Grant had been fascinated with the jurisprudence of broadcast regulation since his law school days in the 1960s. He had written the first historical review and analysis of rulings made by the CRTC and its predecessor, the Board of Broadcast Governors. His biannual compendium of CRTC policies, rulings and related legislation is the bible for other Canadian broadcast lawyers and executives. In the 1970s, Grant had been loaned by his law firm to the CRTC, where he acted as special counsel to the commission in numerous hearings. Following his 1978 return to the firm, he had represented a number of private broadcasters and industry groups as well. There could hardly have been a better proxy for the CRTC—or for hostile intervenors.

Come hearing day Stuart would attend, but it was planned that he would take a seat in the second row. Still deeply mourning the loss of Shirley, he was also recuperating from cancer treatment earlier that year. In a conversation that spring he had been explicit about turning the company's biggest play yet over to his sons. "He finally said, 'Listen, you do what you want,'" Drew recalls. "'It's your application.'" For the first time, "we were the quarterback as opposed to him being the quarterback."

Boyd would join Drew on the front lines. With them in the room, in addition to Stuart and Peter Grant, would be Joanne Levy and Lisa Meeches, Craig news director Al Thorgeirson, sales manager Cam Cowie, comptroller Linda Noto and Hans Jensen, the consultant who had prepared the primary market analysis.

Of them all, Stu was by far the calmest. As the younger men and women worked on their chops and tried to push down their jitters, he had the benefit of having gone through similar tensions countless times in the past. More than that, he had had the comfort of examining his old rival's competing application when it, along with Craig's own, had been publicly gazetted. "As soon as I opened their application, I told the boys, 'We're going to get this thing.' They promised less in 1996 than they did in '93!"

It was true. CanWest had dropped a centrepiece of its application from three years earlier. Then, it had promised something called the Wild Rose Fund which, had the company been licensed, would have spent several million dollars on television production in the province. The fund was missing from CanWest's latest application—a deletion that was in particularly glaring contrast to Craig's proposed A-Channel Drama Fund. So much so, in fact, that after seeing the Craig bid, CanWest had written to the CRTC promising an additional $7 million in production spending. CanWest's late amendment to its application, submitted just days before the scheduled hearings, would be challenged by several intervenors at the hearing as illegal.

In substance, CanWest rested its application almost entirely on the argument that the company needed to own stations in Alberta—as well as in Quebec, where it had other applications before the commission—in order to create a third national television network. Only then, CanWest argued, could it *really* turn the enormous profits it was making to the purpose of producing Canadian shows. Expansively, Izzy Asper promised that licensing his service in the two Alberta cities would bring "clear, unambiguous and quantifiable, tangible and very specific . . . national benefits." As in 1993, CanWest's public declarations assumed—and much of Alberta's business press seemed to accept—that Asper's company held the inside track in the licence competition. "Going in, no one gave us any hope at all," remembers Drew. "People actually said, 'Why would you bother? It's CanWest's to lose. Why would you waste your time, effort and money?' The more people told us that, the more determined we were to find the winning formula."

By the time Team Craig moved out of its Canmore training camp and into the Delta Bow Valley Hotel in Calgary, where the hearings were to begin on July 15, 1996, they believed they had found the formula—and the focus—they sought.

Like most such affairs, the hearings took place in a large, windowless room. A long skirted table backed by several Canadian flags faced other skirted tables and rows of chairs set out for spectators, all under the watchful gaze of television cameras and a separate table of journalists. From a booth off to the side, the background murmer of simultaneous translation followed the public exchanges like a discreet shadow, always just a step behind. For the most part, only the occasional intervenor's recourse to visual aids broke the measured formality of the proceedings. It was the sort of occasion where by mid-afternoon the reporters start pinching themselves to avoid nodding off.

But for the Aspers and the Craigs, this was high noon on the eastern slopes. This was where both teams of broadcasters would step up and show the world exactly what they were made of. It was where the differences between them—their values and business styles as well as their specific undertakings; in a word, their characters—would become crystal clear to those in the room.

The only jury that truly mattered, however, was the CRTC panel itself. On the gavel was Fernand Belisle, a Sudbury native who had risen to the senior executive ranks of Quebec's Telemedia Inc. before being named to the CRTC in 1977. He had been its vice-chairman for broadcasting since 1990. Another panellist to watch was Peter Senchuk, the regional commissioner for Alberta; a veteran broadcaster, he had started out as a station engineer in Dauphin, Manitoba, and worked in Ontario and Saskatchewan before completing his pre-CRTC career in educational TV in Alberta. Also on the panel were David Colville, formerly a communications policy technocrat in the Maritimes, and Garth Dawley, a former CBC television journalist.

CanWest went first. Beaming and effusive as always, Izzy engulfed the panel in a warm, maple-flavoured mist of patriotic aspiration. "For us," he intoned, "this is a historic moment of profound importance in Canadian broadcasting." CanWest's chairman invited the commission to take "the next steps into the exciting future" with him, to join him in "a dream" and in "the fulfillment of that vision" by taking part in the building of a "new Canadian paradigm . . . the foundation of a . . . third new national voice." His opening remarks concluded on an almost biblical note. "Mr. Chairman," Asper ended, "there is a time when it is right to build anew, and this is that time for us."

Other CanWest presenters filled in the details of the "unambiguous and quantifiable" benefits that would flow from the CRTC's decision to license the company in Alberta. CanWest's new stations would produce nine new hours a week of news, four hours of sports, and three and a half hours of "other local productions covering Aboriginal issues, the arts, Alberta business and much more." Anchor Peter Kent was there in person, to note that they would also carry Global's national nightly newscast, produced in Toronto.

"CanWest Alberta will sign on," promised Loren Mawhinney, CanWest's vice-president of Canadian productions, "with no less than an average of seven hours per week of prime time Canadian programming in these [drama, music and dance, and variety] categories." Specifically, Mawhinney asserted, CanWest would deliver four hours of Canadian drama each week, twenty-six half-hours of original children's programming to be purchased from Alberta producers, and more than $4 million over the life of the licence to be spent "nationally" on script development.

The reporters who remained awake sat up in their chairs, pens flying to catch the impressive-sounding figures.

The much smaller Craig team's presentation could not hope to match CanWest's for flamboyance. Not that Drew didn't try a little rhetoric of his own. "Our proposed A-Channel," he began, "will be television for Albertans ... focussed, exciting, relevant and made for Albertans. Our operating philosophy can be summarized in three words: innovative, interactive and independent."

But there was more fibre and sinew than airy philosophy in the Craig presentation. In detail, Thorgeirson explained that A-Channel would deliver seventeen hours of news each week, from *each* of the Calgary and Edmonton stations, thirty-four hours in total, compared with CanWest's weekly seven. To meet that goal, Craig proposed to hire a combined news staff for the two stations larger than CanWest's total staff commitment. Fully one-half of prime-time programming would be Canadian—*every night*. That would rise to 60 per cent on evenings promoted as "Canadian Movie Nights." New local programming would include separate week-nightly shows in each of the two cities covering arts and entertainment and, in a Web-accessible, town-hall format, current affairs. Lisa Meeches told the panellists that her highly successful *The Sharing Circle* program, already seen by 13,000 viewers in Manitoba each week, would create thirty-nine brand-new episodes each season in each of the two cities, examining "the accomplishments of natives, aboriginal history, important issues affecting native people and shared traditions, practices and beliefs."

Coming to what he hoped was the application's trump card, Drew reminded the CRTC panel of the commission's oft-stated concern about the relatively small amount of money most broadcasters spent—on average, only 11 per cent of their Canadian program expenditure—on drama. "We propose to spend over 30 per cent of our Canadian program budget on Canadian drama," Drew informed the panel.

The clutch of independent film and television producers sitting in the audience came to attention as Joanne Levy expanded on A-Channel's proposals. "Just four months ago," Levy recalled for the panel, "the provincial government in Alberta killed its financial support to the production industry. The former provincial agency known as AMPDC [the Alberta Motion Picture Development Corporation] had been one of the most significant factors in the development of the Alberta independent production industry. Now it is gone."

A-Channel, Levy told the panel, was ready to commit $14 million—more cash than the provincial agency had deployed during its entire six-year existence—to fill the agency's place. The drama fund, moreover, would buy national broadcast rights to the productions it funded. That was critical. In the patchwork world of Canadian film financing, that national rights commitment would give producers the green light they needed to secure further funding from national agencies such as Telefilm Canada. A-Channel's investment would focus on the type of programming usually most difficult to finance: long-form drama. Levy believed that the $14 million A-Channel was committing would be enough to see as many as forty movies made in Alberta during the seven-year term of the licence. A-Channel, she added, would be pleased to air them all.

There was one other proposal the Craig team wanted to put before the commission. It had nothing to do with programming, but everything to do with the Craigs's experience as small-town broadcasters for close to half a century. Like CanWest, their application included requests for rebroads in Alberta's two smaller centres, Lethbridge and Red Deer. Permission to include the two smaller cities in their coverage would put any new Craig or CanWest station on the same footing in the market as the two Baton/Electrohome CTV stations. But, Boyd told the panel, Craig recognized that this arrangement would also put pressure on the program services sustained by local advertising on existing rebroads in the two small markets. "We speak with authority on this issue," Boyd noted wryly for the panel, "because we have faced exactly the same situation in Brandon." To lessen that impact, Craig offered its local avails in both cities, at no cost, to the local broadcasters for resale—an offer close to Stu's old "beautiful deal" with Winnipeg's Moffats. (Alternatively, Boyd added, Craig was prepared to forgo rebroads in either small market, if the CRTC considered them impediments to entry into Calgary and Edmonton.)

On subsequent days, the A-Channel team and the team from CanWest each had the opportunity to "intervene" against the other's application. In turn, both did their diligent best to damn the other's competence and candour—drawing to the commission's attention each shortcoming, inadequacy, inconsistency or inflated promise they could uncover in their rival's statements. That was to be expected. What perhaps was not was the imbalance in the attacks levelled against the two applications by other intervenors. Had the Craigs wished, they could almost have sat this round out. The incumbent Alberta broadcasters and other third-party intervenors did their job for them.

Dispassionately, Grant Buchanan, representing WIC Television, licencee of Edmonton's CITV-TV and Calgary's CICT-TV, registered his company's formal opposition to *both* applications. Then he went on to parse, in precise terms, the "fantasy," "illusion," and "smoke and mirrors" of CanWest's promises. Again and again, Buchanan showed CanWest's "new" commitments to be no more than cumulative restatements of what it was already committed to spend through its individual stations, topped up here and there by a pro-rata amount based on Alberta's expected contribution to CanWest revenues. CanWest's $4-million commitment to Canadian script development, under Buchanan's scrutiny, turned out to consist of a meagre $14,000 a year in new money added to CanWest's existing commitments—less than the coffee budget for one of its stations. "In dollar terms," Buchanan said, "CanWest is promising no new incremental benefits at all. Its much referenced national benefits constitute nothing more than simply adding up what its current and proposed stations would be expected to spend in the normal course of business." Its commitments, moreover, were almost all to "Canadian" programming—seldom to "Alberta" production (apart from the commitment to buy some children's series from producers in the province). "CanWest has made it very clear," he said, "that its current applications for new stations in Alberta are not really about service to Alberta at all."

Warming to his work, Buchanan moved on to the "notion," encouraged by CanWest's executives, "that it is ... un-Canadian to oppose CanWest's purveying of U.S. programs to Canadians coast-to-coast." He reminded the panel of the words in the Broadcasting Act that describe radio and television as "a public service essential to the maintenance and enhancement of national identity and cultural sovereignty," and which require broadcasters "to safeguard, enrich and strengthen the cultural, political, social and economic fabric of Canada."

"Can the CanWest application stand up to that test?" Buchanan demanded to know. "Global may indeed have greatly increased its profitability since coming under the exclusive control of CanWest," he noted, "but it has not increased the viewership of Canadian programming by Canadians on Global. Since 1990, Global has yet to match the audience it delivered for Canadian programs in 1988 [when Asper gained control of the Ontario network]." CanWest, he showed, spent less than half as much money on Canadian programming—measured by percentage of revenue—as CTV did. In fact, it spent less in absolute dollars as well, although CanWest was about three times as profitable as the original private network. "CanWest currently spends a lower percentage on Canadian programming than any other major component in the system," the WIC executive told the CRTC. Moreover, Buchanan warned, CanWest's "plummeting spending and skyrocketing revenues driven by U.S. programs" could, if it also received Alberta licences, grant Asper's company "a permanent structural advantage, in controlling the top foreign programs on Canadian television."

The official transcript of Grant Buchanan's intervention against the two licence applications before the CRTC panel runs to thirty-four typed pages. Of those, thirty-two are taken up with his excoriation of CanWest. Slightly less than two pages record Buchanan's complaints about the Craig application. His main worry was that their new station might be *too* successful, that the Craigs might have "over-estimated the size of the Alberta market; and therefore, under-estimated the harm that their arrival would cause." After that passing jibe, he returned to burying CanWest.

Other interventions, even those that were nominally opposed to both companies—or neither—followed much the same pattern. A brief submitted by the Alberta Motion Picture Industries Association, for instance, was scrupulous in noting that "we have chosen not to intervene positively or negatively on either application." Its comments on the competing proposals, however, were telling. "The CanWest Global application," the association's executive director, Leon Lubin, observed, "does little to respond to the predicament of Alberta producers after the demise of the AMPDC. CanWest has committed $375,000 to the development of Alberta projects over the seven year licence period. This . . . will be managed out of Toronto. In the experience of AMPIA producers, we dare not anticipate an Albertan presence on the CanWest 'system.'"

The association analyzed the Craig proposal quite differently. "The A-Channel commitment to spend two million dollars annually on Albertan development and production," it noted, "will go a long way to helping Alberta's indigenous industry stay on track with its current pattern of growth. It also reflects a belief in the industry and its ability to continue producing world class programming. Although A-Channel is not a link in a national 'system,' it is willing to purchase national broadcast rights, which it will then resell across the country. [It] would provide a much-needed broadcast outlet for Canadian feature films."

Other intervenors did not even pretend to neutrality. Appearing for the CTV network, its president and CEO John Cassaday spent several minutes objecting to the prospect of CanWest getting the same sort of "structural" advantages from the award of Alberta licences that Buchanan had feared. Cassaday made it clear, however, that CTV was "not intervening against the Craig application."

CHUM's Moses Znaimer went even further. The guru of CITY-TV's Queen Street citadel in Toronto took aim first at CanWest's last-minute enrichment of its proposals after the applications had been published in the *Canada Gazette*. The rule against such under-the-wire salting of applications, Znaimer noted, existed "so that interested parties and the general public can have a fair opportunity to assess and comment." If it were allowed, he predicted, "proceedings would become chaotic, as no two parties would be talking about the same thing."

Then Znaimer reminded the CRTC panel that it had called for applications for service in Alberta. "CanWest's stated goal," Znaimer observed, "is to amortize existing Global programming on a third national English-language network. Local service to residents of Alberta is quite secondary. Therefore, we do not believe that CanWest has met the call."

"At the same time," Znaimer continued, "we believe the Commission has an application before it which does respond to that call." After a lengthy comparison of Craig's commitments to CanWest's, Znaimer concluded his remarks: "The application by Craig Broadcast Systems best fulfills the criteria set out in the call and will provide by far the better, more truly local alternative and complementary television service to Albertans."

By the end of three days of hearings, the credibility of CanWest's application had been challenged. The Craigs stood accused of being possibly a little too competitive for the complete comfort of the incumbents in the country's richest TV market.

Then came the final act, the closing "rebuttals" by each applicant to the interventions against them. There was a strict, ten-minute procedural time limit on each party's remarks.

The CanWest side did not even attempt to keep to the time limit. Its entire platoon of suits, Global's hunky Peter Kent among them alongside the somewhat less hunky David and Leonard Asper, paraded back into the Delta Bow Valley meeting room. Beginning with an address by Jim Sward, president-designate of CanWest's proposed Alberta subsidiary, the ten-minute rebuttal period expanded elastically into a thirty-minute round robin of CanWest executives' weighty last words. Finally, Sward summed up: "Mr. Chairman, that is what it is all about, it is about dreams, and it is about aspirations. And we have a dream and an optimistic attitude and a belief in our ability to accomplish it and a great love for this country. All we need is your approval to get on with that dream."

It was pure Izzyvision—and a perfect note on which to close. Only Sward didn't end there. In a choreographed outburst that must stand as one of the strangest breaches of CRTC procedural decorum on record, the CanWest executive handed the microphone over to David Asper. Earlier in the performance, David's brother Leonard had compared CanWest's desire for a third national television network to the heroic completion of the transcontinental railroad. "This application," Leonard had instructed the panel, "is about rewarding the builders of the railroad." Now, David launched into a maudlin refrain on CanWest's manifest destiny in which Izzy Asper's name, and references to the family succession at CanWest, surfaced more than a dozen times in the course of yet another ten minutes.

Drew Craig's rebuttal took precisely ten minutes. He had timed it repeatedly to make certain that it did. It stuck tightly to the small number of criticisms levelled at the A-Channel application during the interventions, concisely answering each one. Drew restated Craig's contention that it could enter the Alberta market in a "gradual and orderly" way that posed no threat to incumbent broadcasters. He underlined the company's commitment to "provide real dollars . . . at 20 per cent of budget" for Alberta drama productions. He thanked the intervenors who had supported A-Channel's application. He did not once mention that he, his father and his grandfather had been in the broadcasting business slightly more than twice as long as the Aspers had.

When Drew was finished, the CRTC's legal counsel, in a pro forma question, asked whether being on the air within a year of receiving a licence would present the Craigs with any difficulty. Suppressing a smile, Drew answered: "No, it would not."

At last, panel chairman Fernand Belisle asked if Drew had anything else to add.

Drew took a breath, then answered: "I think there is one further point I would like to make. As you know, we were here two years ago, when the application was denied. There were two points cited. One was the ability for the market to absorb a new player, and the second was the A-Channel commitment to drama. I think it has been demonstrated that the market needs and wants a new station. I think that we have stepped up to the plate in terms of our commitment to Canadian drama production."

"We would be very honoured to have these stations here and be Alberta broadcasters," Johnny Craig's eldest grandson finished simply.

Even as Chairman Belisle thanked him and dismissed the Craig team, lawyer Peter Grant leaned over to Drew and, in his ear, murmured: "You've got it!"

The Craigs had no way to know whether Grant's instincts were right. In any case, they had very little time to think about it before shifting gears for the defence of their Vancouver application.

This contest would be very different. Calgary and Edmonton, however distinct in character and pace from Winnipeg, are still flatland cities. The personalities of all three places belong indelibly to the great central plain that sweeps from the Peace River down across 4,800 kilometres of continent to the Gulf of Mexico. The common *Zeitgeist* of the great North American middle fuelled the old jazz circuit that ran, and perhaps still runs, from New Orleans up through Chicago to Winnipeg. It draws the horse trailers on their worn tires south down I-15 from the Eastern Slopes to the rodeo rings of Elko, Nevada, and Wyoming's Cheyenne—"the daddy of them all." It's the reason for the frequent flyers in $1,200 cowboy boots accumulating air miles on shuttle flights between the Alberta and Texas oil patches.

Vancouver is on the edge of the land mass. It looks south, too, but Vancouver's points of reference there are Hollywood, California—home of the movies—and Redmond, Washington—the home of Microsoft. And for many of the city's residents, the real cardinal points are not on this continent at all: they are to the west—the *far* west—in China, southeast Asia and northern India. By the turn of the century, close to 40 per cent of Vancouver's residents belonged to multicultural minorities. The largest numbers were Chinese (speaking either Mandarin or Cantonese) and South Asians (with Punjabi-speaking Sikhs the most numerous among them).

Pretty much no one in Vancouver knew where Brandon was.

There was another difference. This would be no shoot-out at the Delta Bow Valley Hotel, no duel where two applicants went *mano a mano,* brief to brief. The last time the CRTC had opened the door on the Vancouver market had been twenty-three years earlier, when the commission had licensed CKVU-TV. With local broadcasters earning profit margins (before interest and taxes) of close to 30 per cent on revenues—twice the industry average—the 1996 call had them lining up at the gate. In all, there were five applications before the CRTC for Vancouver. And here, Izzy Asper was a long way from being the acknowledged front-runner.

The golden boy this time around was Moses Znaimer. The CHUM Television president had tried before to establish a foothold on the West Coast. In the 1970s, he had contested the "third-service" licence that went instead to CKVU. This time, he was promising to bring CITY-TV's edgy, urban, in-your-face style to Vancouver. With his willingness to explore the creative metaphysics of the broadcasting business, and his strangely compelling charisma, Znaimer played well with Vancouver's TV critics and arts community. In a coup that he may have come to regret, he even persuaded then premier Glen Clark to appear in a cameo turn on CHUM's promotional video, endorsing its bid. Through the weeks before the September hearings and afterwards, whenever the press ran a comparison of the competing applications, CHUM's would be rated the "critics' choice."

Asper, in fact, was technically not asking for a Vancouver licence at all. CanWest was asking to be licensed in Victoria. Its service there, it insisted, would be substantially different from what it already aired on CKVU-TV in Vancouver (which could also be seen in Victoria). There would be fifteen hours a week of local news and another ten hours a week of local variety, business and politics. CanWest pointed to the precedent set by WIC, which had stations in both B.C. cities. But as Vancouver *Province* TV reporter Mike Roberts noted skeptically in a comparison of CanWest's application against its rivals: "There are 2.3 million people in the lower mainland and only 650,000 on the island. You do the math."

Rogers Broadcasting—the telecommunication and cable conglomerate's radio and TV wing—proposed an ingenious twist on the same manoeuvre CanWest had employed to turn KCND-TV, Pembina, into CKND-TV, Winnipeg. Many multicultural viewers in Vancouver already watched a pay-TV service called Talentvision, owned by a tough-minded, Taiwanese-born investor/developer named Thomas Fung. Rogers was asking the CRTC for permission to buy the assets of Talentvision and transform them into an off-the-air broadcast service modelled loosely on its existing CFMT-TV in Toronto. Whatever its other merits, Rogers's plan would allow it to get into the market for as little half what some of its rivals (including Craig) were prepared to pay.

Baton's bid was harder to peg than those of either Rogers or CHUM. Its Vancouver Television (VTV) application proposed a program mix not very different from the one already playing on WIC's CHAN-TV. But CHAN was the local affiliate of the network Ivan Fecan had in his sights: if he bagged CTV, he would end up being the network programmer for his cross-town rival. By the same token, whatever programming Baton bought for use on its CTV station could not air on VTV. Nonetheless, Fecan's application offered solid mainstream English programming and brought with it Baton's long record of Canadian production.

Craig Broadcast made scarcely a blip on the Vancouver media's radar. "Virtually unknown on the West Coast," observed one reviewer. "Considered the long shot," another echoed.

The easy dismissal that greeted the proposed VITV, Vancouver Independent Television, was not only unfortunate. It was careless. By many objective measures, Craig Broadcast had put more on the table than any other applicant. The crudest of those was the bottom line: the total amount of money each player was prepared to commit to starting a new station. For Craig and its partners, that amount was $22 million (about as much as it had budgeted for *both* Alberta stations). Baton and CHUM were in the ballpark but trailing, having promised $21 and $20 million respectively to a Vancouver licence. CanWest's step-out of CKVU would cost it only $15 million. Rogers planned to spend $11 million to buy Talentvision.

But it wasn't just the money. It was where the money was going. As they had done in Alberta, the Craigs put forward a taboo-breaking notion for a Canadian television station: a program schedule in which Canadian programs weren't the exception, they were the rule. There would be a sassy, nightly downtown arts-and-entertainment show called *Yaletown*. There would be a weekly *Sharing Circle* for the lower mainland's least-served minority: native Canadians. There would be more microwave trucks for reporting live news than CITY-TV owned in Toronto; and the six o'clock news would come in Punjabi, Chinese *and* English, in the hope of breaking down cultural barriers as well as forging a distinct identity in the marketplace.

There would be $14 million for long-form drama projects by Vancouver producers. The equivalent of the A-Channel Drama Fund in Alberta, it would give B.C. producers an alternative to the all-too-familiar, and properly resented, pilgrimage to Toronto for a "$2,000 cup of coffee" with some programmer from CBC, CTV or Global who might give their project a green light.

Overall, 60 per cent of the new station's air time would be devoted to Canadian programs. Forty per cent of its revenue would be spent on Canadian programs: $83 million over the seven-year term of the licence. The next-highest commitments (from Baton and CHUM) came in $9 million lower.

However distracted they may have been by Shirley's unexpected death, the Craig boys made no apologies for what they hoped to do in Vancouver. In fact, Drew confides, "I felt it was better than our Alberta application."

In late September, the Craig team checked into the Pan Pacific Hotel on Vancouver's waterfront, part of the gleaming white complex whose striking, sail-like profile has become as much a symbol of the city as Toronto's CN Tower. They rehearsed as seriously as they had in Canmore, but these hearings lacked the drama that had hung over the Delta Bow Valley. These were closer to round-robin appearances before the Inquisition, with each applicant in turn subject to an exquisitely polite grilling. By the end of the last day, the Craigs would feel that they had held their own and made their case.

Beyond that, it was anyone's guess. Even after a score of appearances before the CRTC, says Drew Craig, "You really don't know, when you walk out of the room, whether you won or lost."

On November 1, the Craigs learned they had won—in Alberta.

It would be two more months before they heard they had lost in Vancouver. The CRTC gave that licence to Baton. Reviewing events later, Drew says, the Craigs came to the realization that "when we appeared before the Commission in Vancouver, they had already given us the licence for Alberta. We didn't know that. They did.

"It was a gutsy move to give us Alberta. It would have been a really, really gutsy move to give us Alberta *and* B.C."

As it was, the Craigs were about to face the fight of their lives just to hold on to what they *had* won.

12

Hold the Champagne

Somehow, the fizz seemed to go out of the champagne.

Stuart was still buoyant, savouring the cool effervescence of the bubbly as he contemplated the text of the CRTC's decision. Dated that day, November 1, 1996, it awarded television licences in Calgary and Edmonton to Craig Broadcast Systems.

"Based on its assessment of the application and of all other available evidence," the CRTC had written, "the Commission is convinced that the applications by A-Channel are superior to those by CanWest."

Stu smiled his three-cornered grin and sipped some more champagne. But Drew, Boyd and Miles were crestfallen, to put it mildly. Within minutes of the joyful news from Ottawa had come an astonishing press release, from CanWest Global Communications.

The commission had confirmed what the Craigs already knew: theirs was the better proposal. Single-handedly, A-Channel was going to rescue the Alberta film industry from asphyxiation in the anoxia left behind by the withdrawal of provincial funding. A-Channel was ready to produce three hours of local Alberta news for every two CanWest promised (it had budgeted eight live-remote trucks for the purpose; CanWest, none). A-Channel had guaranteed at least $14 million to make movies in Alberta for national distribution; CanWest offered half as much. A-Channel's schedule contained sixty-three hours a week of local programming; CanWest's, forty. The rest of the A-Channel line-up was going, perforce (WIC's independent stations already relying on CanWest Global's roster of U.S. hits), to bring new shows to Alberta TV screens. CanWest had merely proposed to move its American line-up down the street from the WIC stations to its own, leaving those long-standing broadcasters to scramble for something else to air.

Yet somehow, Izzy Asper found it "inexplicable" that the CRTC had granted a licence to Craig Broadcast, instead of to him. The press release from CanWest Global fairly steamed with injured virtue and high dudgeon. More troubling, Asper's release declared: "It is our intention to petition the federal cabinet to review and set aside this decision. If it is successful, the CRTC will be required to re-hear Can-West's application."

"It was devastating for us," Drew says. There were a thousand demands that needed to be met to get the new stations up and running by their target date ten months hence. New staff, from general managers on down, buildings, cameras, transmitters—and somewhere to *put* the transmitters. Programs! Joanne Levy's phone was already ringing off the hook with Alberta producers eager to bite into the A-Channel Drama Fund; now she had to tell them there might not *be* a Drama Fund, if CanWest got its way. Until the petition was dropped or disposed of, Drew recognized, "We couldn't make a single decision."

A second nasty surprise came less than a week later, in the form of a blast from the past named Samy Salloum—the Edmonton lawyer who represented David Mackenzie. It was the Wednesday after the Friday decision when Stuart picked up the phone in Brandon to hear Salloum's greeting. Salloum came quickly to the point. His client congratulated Craig on winning the Alberta licences. Now, Salloum explained, Mackenzie wished to execute the memorandum of understanding signed—and abandoned—three years earlier for the purpose of the last application and assume "his" 30 per cent interest in the new Alberta television stations.

Stu was dumbfounded. But not speechless. "We just said: 'Sorry, boys!'"

Two days later, Salloum faxed a letter to Craig's Toronto lawyer, Peter Grant, advising him of Salloum's intention to prepare "pleadings for such injunctive and other relief as we deem appropriate and before such courts or tribunals as we deem fit." When this legal threat was ultimately carried out, the formal document issued by a clerk of the Court of Queen's Bench of Alberta and served on the Craigs would be rather more direct. "You have been sued," it read. "You are the defendant."

But that was a battle for another day. The skilled solicitors of McCarthy Tétrault would have no trouble holding Salloum off for a little while at least. The more immediate threat was Izzy.

In Asper's self-published history of his company's first two decades, there is a photograph of the former Manitoba Liberal Leader (cigarette in one hand, drink in the other) proudly accompanying then prime minister Pierre Trudeau into a trade meeting in the early 1970s. Since then, the Minnedosa lawyer had never stopped adding to his political Rolodex. By the nineties, Asper's name was on every seriously ambitious Liberal's list of must-court power brokers. He was a founding patron of the career of Foreign Affairs Minister Lloyd Axworthy, the Member of Parliament for the riding of Winnipeg South Centre.

"Izzy's been an old soldier for the Liberal Party for a lot of years. He decided he'd try to use political influence to win what he couldn't win in public before the commission," says Drew Craig.

It would be touch and go.

CanWest presented its formal petition to Jocelyne Bourgon, the Clerk of the Privy Council and Secretary to Cabinet, on the eighteenth of November. The portentous twenty-four-page document, submitted over the signature of James Sward, the president of CanWest Alberta Television, was a confabulation of bluster and contempt for the smaller Brandon company. "Those who are familiar with . . . Canadian broadcasting," Sward opened, were "shocked and dismayed by the Commission's decision." The CRTC's judgement "defied any reasonably applied principles of logic," was an "error" that made "no sense," and was "clearly contrary to the needs and interests of Albertans and other Canadians."

The heart of CanWest's case, as it had been throughout the battle for Alberta, was that the national interest would be served only by CanWest becoming even bigger and richer than it already was. "This is not just about Calgary and Edmonton," the brief argued. "It is about the very future of Canadian broadcasting. [The CRTC decision] destined the Canadian television production industry to long-term domination by foreign broadcasting companies."

Canada, the petition observed, "is one of the few developed nations with fewer than three national, over-the-air, television networks." Without such a "third voice," CanWest asserted, Canadian television was doomed to become a wasteland of second-rate "purely local" fare under a cataclysmic flood of American entertainment. "We must recognize," Sward's jeremiad read, "that, in a metaphorical sense, the 'barbarians are at the gate.' Foreign media conglomerates have no sympathy with Canadian cultural sovereignty. To the executives of these companies, Canadians are just 'Americans with sweaters': if we cannot compete with them, they will 'eat us alive.'"

Like General Motors and America in the Eisenhower years, what was good for CanWest was good for the Maple Leaf. "U.S. services are 'coming over the wall' and are meeting little or no resistance," Sward continued. "What Canada needs at this critical moment in its historical development is more national institutions and 'ties that bind,' not less. If there is to be any hope of creating a national sense of pride and identity, Canadians must be able to see and talk to one another through national institutions. "Only CanWest might have had the economies of scale necessary to compete with foreign broadcast companies that are stampeding into our market." *Might have,* that is, had it not been for the "grievous" failure of the CRTC to do its plain duty to Crown and country.

To broadcasters familiar with Global's minimal contribution over the years to Canadian programming, the notion of CanWest now dressing itself in the costume of Captain Canuck was, well, laughable. So was the argument that CanWest needed to own licences in Alberta, either in order to create a program network or to air its shows there. Every Canadian show that CanWest Global produced (other than its Ontario regional news) already *was* being aired in Alberta. And CanWest had been free for years—was, indeed, still free—to apply to become a network, just as CTV had in the mid-sixties, when it was no more than a cooperative of six stations all controlled by different owners.

Whether or not Canadian culture is under seige is an argument preserved under glass to keep academics in Ph.D. story-lines while Celine Dion buys another chateau in Tuscany. There is no denying the inbound flood of American culture. But the "swarm" of invading broadcasters that CanWest was crying out alarm over was nowhere to be seen, and for a very good reason. In Canada, as in the United States, foreigners are forbidden from owning broadcasting licences.

CanWest's argument that Canada needed a third, commonly owned television network—either to fight off foreign broadcasters or to hold its head up among democracies—rested on bad assumptions and worse logic. In light of the common rule of thumb that Canada's population, and hence its capacity to support services, is one-tenth that of the United States, CanWest's own comparison with the six commercial networks operating south of the border (ABC, CBS, NBC, FOX, UPN and Warner Brothers) might have suggested that in fact Canadians were lucky to have even one network, let alone two officially licensed in both English and French, plus several large "station groups."

CanWest's brief also neglected to mention two salient facts about those U.S. "networks." One, that none actually owned more than a handful of the stations on its chain. And two, that U.S. law explicitly *forbids* any single owner from holding broadcast stations covering more than 35 per cent of the American population. Were that standard in effect in Canada, Asper would have had to divest half the stations he already owned.

The portions of the brief that dealt with the Craigs's commitments and CanWest's own were similarly riddled with inaccurate assertions, significant omissions and loaded language. At one point, CanWest declared that the commission's decision "slams the door shut" on $165 million in national production commitments CanWest had offered in exchange for its licence. The figure it had used in Calgary was $120 million (although even that, on examination, had proven not to be new money at all, but barely more than what CanWest Global had committed in order to secure the renewal of the licences it already had). There was no mention whatsoever of the $14-million A-Channel Drama Fund. Other assertions, notably that Craig would produce "inferior" programs "of little interest to other Canadians," were simply insulting—as much to Alberta's professional community of writers, producers and performers as to the boys from Brandon.

But the Cabinet committee that would weigh CanWest's appeal was not made up of broadcasters. It was made up of politicians keenly attuned to the resonance of any appeal to national sovereignty. Few, if any, would be familiar with the complex cross-currents of broadcast commerce and policy. (An exception might be its chairperson, Heritage Minister Sheila Copps.) It would be especially difficult to counter CanWest Global's inflated claims for the "national benefits" its third network might create. The company's various briefs, pleadings and licence applications shuffled, restated, amalgamated and sub-allocated its Canadian-content spending commitments from station to station so often that the effect was like keeping track of a pea under so many walnut shells.

Back in Brandon, Stuart was ready for the fight—and more confident than any of his sons. "The boys were more worried about it than I was," he would say later. "I didn't think he had a hope in hell." For one thing, "there was an election coming up and we had a lot of friends too." Stuart had never been as deeply involved in politics as his father;

some Liberals even suspected him of harbouring Tory leanings. But among the third generation of Craigs, Boyd, in particular, took a lively interest in issues beyond broadcasting. He was rapidly becoming a significant donor to Liberal fund-raising campaigns. Added Stuart: "We had a lot of support from Liberals in Alberta."

Craig Broadcast had two other aces to play: Peter Grant and the facts.

Grant's own partisanship was either so discreet or so nonexistent that he was repeatedly chosen by rival federal parties to divvy up the political air time they received under the Elections Act. Nonetheless, he knew how power flowed through Ottawa's corridors, and he quickly framed a strategy to get the facts to the front of the debate. His first advice to the Craigs: hire a lobbyist.

That proved more easily said than done. Whether through design or simply the extent of its many interests, CanWest seemed to have a contract with every lobbyist the Craigs called on. One after another, they regretted to inform the Brandon broadcasters that they were prevented, by rules of conflict, from accepting the Craig file. Finally, the Ottawa-based Capital Hill Group took on the case. They identified who would be on the Cabinet committee considering CanWest's appeal and began lining up appointments.

"We worked completely differently from how CanWest worked," says Drew. "They worked from the prime minister's office down. We worked from the staff level up. We spent a couple of months tramping around in snowbanks buying lunch for anybody who'd talk to us."

Meetings were held with senior policy advisors and executive assistants to key Alberta ministers who would be certain to be in the decision-making loop on a file with such visibility in the province, as well as those whose departmental interests were involved. Among them were staff working for Copps and for Anne McLellan (at the time Minister of Natural Resources and, more importantly, a rising star who represented Edmonton West), Senator Dan Hays (then president of the Liberal Party of Canada), Solicitor General Herb Gray, Revenue Minister Jane Stewart, Government Senate Leader Joyce Fairbairn, Human Resources Minister Pierre Pettigrew, Indian Affairs and Northern Development Minister Ron Irwin and Minister of Intergovernmental Affairs Stéphane Dion. Liz Mulholland, a senior policy analyst to the prime minister, was also briefed.

With them all, Drew and Stuart Craig, Peter Grant and Capital Hill's Herb Metcalfe made the same three core points:

1. CanWest did not need to own stations in Alberta to achieve its stated goals.
2. The commission had given full and fair consideration to CanWest's "national commitments" at the Calgary hearing.
3. Stripped of rhetoric, the CanWest commitments were materially and demonstrably inferior to those of Craig Broadcast Systems.

Exactly as the CRTC had found. There had been no "error."

Craig Broadcast also reached out to a neutral but influential voice for the very community that CanWest was purporting to save: the creators of Canadian film and television. The Craigs realized that many large Canadian television producers would be reluctant to speak out against CanWest: too many relied on contracts with Global for their livelihoods. (Several of the most influential of those producers, however, including Robert Lantos, at the time president of Alliance Communications, a large Toronto-based moviemaker and distributor, had already pointedly refused to endorse CanWest's petition. "Our official and heartfelt policy," Lantos told the Craig camp in a note, "is that any challenge to [the] CRTC's authority undermines the integrity of the CRTC and consequently weakens the Canadian broadcast system and in particular the production side. We will not contribute to any effort, such as this one, which could result in a more vulnerable CRTC.")

What the Craig side *was* able to line up was a strongly worded intervention letter to Cabinet from the Directors' Guild of Canada. Its 2,000 members were not the men and women who would have to go to Global the day after Cabinet ruled and ask for money. But they were intimately familiar with where that money went—and where it was needed. The guild had done a detailed analysis of the Craig and CanWest bids before the Calgary hearings and had appeared there to tell the CRTC: "By every important standard we applied in assessing the applications, the Craig applications are not only better—but are superior by a wide margin." Now, the guild restated that conclusion in a letter to Bourgon and urged the federal Cabinet to confirm the CRTC's decision.

But CanWest had not been idle either. In public, CanWest Alberta Television president Jim Sward may have done his side more harm than good when he appeared, in several interviews in November, to threaten that the country's wealthiest and most profitable broadcaster would have to cancel such popular Canadian shows as *Traders* and *Jake and the Kid* (a made-in-Alberta series) if its petition were denied. But from their own lobbying efforts, the Craigs soon learned that Asper's pitch to his political contacts was more carrot than stick. "Give me another hearing," Izzy was saying, "and I'll put more on the table."

By late November, with Asper knocking on doors in Edmonton as well as Ottawa, Peter Grant made a risky suggestion. "I wonder," he wrote Drew, "if we should not bring the debate out into the open." Drew talked it over with Stu, Boyd and Miles. They agreed, Drew says. "We had to pull this out of the backrooms."

The Craigs made their move. It hit readers of the Calgary *Herald* and the Edmonton *Journal* right between the eyes on the morning of Friday, December 6, 1996: a full-page ad urging readers, in a half-page headline, to "Tell Ottawa the CRTC made the right decision." The rest of the ad presented readers with reasons why they should do so, and a chart showing the commitments of the two candidates. Side by side like that, the comparison left little doubt that the commission had, indeed, "made the right decision."

From Calgary, Brandon and Portage la Prairie, the members of the Craig team again contacted, either by letter or in person, everyone who had expressed support for either of their applications—A-Channel in Alberta or Vancouver Independent Television—and asked them now to support the integrity of the process they had participated in by writing to Cabinet to endorse the CRTC's decision.

Soon, they began to get feedback from their contacts in Ottawa. If nothing else, the Craig ad had significantly raised the profile of CanWest's application on the radar of the nation's capital. "It became apparent this was a political issue," recalls Drew. "We got the impression it made the politicians antsy." But the expressions of support from critical constituencies were beginning to appear. On January 7, with Cabinet's legal deadline for ruling on the petition just three weeks away, they ran the ad again—this time in the national pages of the *Globe and Mail*.

Days later, Drew received a telephone call from one of the people he'd gotten to know during his many meetings over the last two months in the shadow of the Peace Tower. In retrospect, the scene sounds like a bad parody of *All the President's Men*. "CBC is doing a story on you on *Venture*," the source confided. "And you should be worried."

For folks whose business was broadcasting, there should have been nothing alarming about being on the receiving end of a piece of TV journalism. But like most businesspeople—stage-centre characters like Asper and Znaimer being the exception even in broadcasting—the

Craigs had never gone out of their way to court media attention. In their forays beyond Manitoba, the family had fallen into the long media shadows cast by more flamboyant rivals. The thumbnail descriptive reporters relied on most when covering the Craigs in Alberta and Vancouver was the less than illuminating "little-known." The Craigs were savvy enough to understand that whatever spin *Venture* chose to put on their case would define Craig Broadcast Systems for much of the public.

There was really only one course that held out hope of an upside: the Craigs decided to put their trust in the professionalism of the *Venture* crew. A producer from the program had contacted Drew months earlier about doing a story but appeared to have lost interest. Now Drew dug the contact out of his files and placed a call himself. *Venture* was indeed looking at the Craig/CanWest feud and wanted to spend some time with the Craigs. Drew invited the program to come to Brandon to interview Stuart, but apologized that he himself would be in New Orleans during the days the *Venture* crew suggested, attending the annual National Association of Television Producers trade show at which independent program vendors pitch their wares. "That's okay," the show's producer said, "we'll go there."

CanWest's chairman Izzy Asper, the Craigs would later learn, had refused *Venture* an interview, although the program crew did manage to catch Asper's son David for a comment at the same New Orleans trade show. (As telecast, the younger Asper stuck close to the CanWest script, insinuating that Craig Broadcast was not up to the task of meeting its commitments.)

The deadline in law for the federal Cabinet to rule on CanWest's petition was January 29, 1997—ninety days after the CRTC had released its decision. The Cabinet committee that would recommend a course of action to the full body, with Copps sitting as chair, was to meet on January 28, a Tuesday. *Venture* was scheduled to air on CKX, as well as the rest of the CBC network, on Sunday, January 26.

The item on Craig and CanWest led the show. It said little about the respective merits of the two groups' Alberta applications. But neither did it play the Craigs for rubes. If there was a certain David and Goliath quality to the contest that correspondent Haver Gould portrayed, it was clear that David was far from outclassed. The item brought attention to Craig's ground-breaking venture into MDS wireless cable and gave Drew the opportunity to underscore the Craig record for delivering on its licence commitments. Craig might not be as well known a name as CanWest, but Stuart had confidently told Gould, with that grin of his: "You're going to hear more from us."

The next morning, the Cabinet committee voted. Shortly before noon, the telephone rang in Drew Craig's Portage la Prairie office. A voice asked him to hold for the Minister of Heritage.

The line went quiet for a moment as the Ottawa operator put Drew on hold. He held his breath. The line came to life.

"This is Sheila Copps," a voice said. "I wanted you to hear it from me first." Cabinet had rejected CanWest's petition. The CRTC decision stood. The licences for Calgary and Edmonton were A-Channel's. In public, Copps said it again: "The CRTC decision was upheld—it was a good and valid decision."

This time, no one felt it necessary to hold back their emotions. "We're ecstatic," Drew told reporters. "It restores our faith in the system. It's a fair process."

For Stu, there was particular vindication in the Cabinet verdict. Not only had Craig "won that thing hands down"; just as importantly, the Cabinet had confirmed that "we won it *fair and square.*"

(In a gesture to CanWest, Cabinet also directed the CRTC to re-examine the need for a third national network. Asper declared this "precisely what we have been seeking" and added, "Our main objective in this appeal has been achieved." Two plus two, it seemed, had once again equalled six.)

Drew, who planned to move with Jodi and the kids to Calgary to oversee the launch of A-Channel, had suffered a two-and-a-half-month delay in getting started. With September now only eight months away, the new service had just three employees: Joanne Levy, Jodi and himself. With mental lists of things-to-do swirling through his head, Drew set to work. In a decision that Johnny B. would have deeply approved, Drew persuaded Stu and his brothers that their two new stations should not only have everything they had promised in the application: they should also be Canada's first *all-digital* television studios. Of course.

Meanwhile, the Mackenzie litigation was moving through the courts. Stuart and Peter Grant were both summoned to Calgary to be cross-examined on their affidavits.

Mackenzie's claim rested on the Memorandum of Understanding

that he, Stuart and the representative of Midwest Television had signed in October 1993. The memorandum had set out several points of agreement. Among them:

- Mackenzie's Alberta Interactive Multimedia Inc. would withdraw its application for a television licence;
- The application filed by the Craigs with the CRTC under the name "The Alberta Channel Inc." would be amended to include Mackenzie as a minority investor;
- Mackenzie would hold 33 per cent of those shares and nominate three of eight seats on the board of directors. Craig Broadcast would receive 57 per cent of the shares and five seats. Midwest would have 10 per cent and one seat.

But as the Craigs well remembered, it had been Salloum and Mackenzie's demands for a larger role in the management of the planned station that had scuttled all attempts to translate the Memorandum of Understanding into a binding shareholders' agreement. In the subscription documents filed with the CRTC application, it was made clear that the share commitments were dependent on the licence being issued to the applicant. As it was, when the CRTC had decided to award no licence at all in that round, The Alberta Channel fell into corporate limbo. No shares were ever issued. No officers or directors were ever appointed.

The one mistake the Craigs had made, it appeared, was in not taking steps to formally dissolve the half-formed company.

In November of 1994, five months after the CRTC denied all licence applications, Salloum had written to the Craigs. Observing "I do not believe that we formally incorporated The Alberta Channel Inc.," Salloum suggested that both parties write off their respective investments as tax losses.

Prior to submitting the new application in 1996, Stuart Craig had written to Salloum asking permission to use the name and the "A-Channel" logo that had originally been designed by Drew Craig for the 1993 application. Salloum had replied in the positive, adding, "Both Mr. Mackenzie and I wish you every success in your application." Later, Mackenzie had called Drew Craig to ask whether the Craig application was "all partnered up" and, on learning that it was, had let the matter drop. In fact, in the knowledge that Mackenzie was not included as one of the investors, Salloum subsequently submitted a letter to the CRTC supporting the Craig bid.

Nevertheless, in a statement of claim filed with the Alberta Court of Queen's Bench in Edmonton on June 19, 1997, Mackenzie asserted that Stuart Craig, as an officer-designate in The Alberta Channel Inc., had been under an obligation to make the 1996 application under that company name. Instead, Craig had found new partners in TD Capital and Midwest, and sought a licence as A-Channel Inc.

Mackenzie sought the court's leave to commence what in law is known as a "derivative" action, empowering him to sue Stuart (and TD Capital) in the name of The Alberta Channel for allegedly misappropriating the "opportunity" of seeking the licence in 1996. It was a legal argument that required the judge to accept that Mackenzie possessed "derivative" rights to sue on The Alberta Channel's behalf. Alberta's Business Corporations Act defined the categories of people who could make such a claim. They included shareholders, beneficial owners, officers, directors or "any other person who, in the discretion of the court, is a proper person to make an application"—a potentially wide-open definition. But the judge *also* had to accept two other assertions: that the Craigs had concealed the 1996 CRTC call for applications from Mackenzie and that Mackenzie had been acting in good faith himself.

The first was plainly not the case. The applications had been front-page news, and it was evident that Mackenzie had known all about them. At the end of August, just before the stations went on the air, the Honourable Donald H. Medhurst rendered his verdict on the rest of Salloum's pleading. He was prepared to admit that Mackenzie might have had an argument, as an "anticipatory shareholder," that he was a "proper person" to launch a derivative action. But he had disqualified himself on the test of good faith. "The public show of support [for A Channel's application], the private letters of encouragement and the lack of notice of the potential claim until after the granting of the licence strongly suggests that the Mackenzie Parties were 'laying in the weeds' and waiting to take advantage of the Craigs' efforts," Medhurst wrote in his judgement. "Leave to pursue a derivative action . . . is denied."

Salloum would appeal that ruling on behalf of Mackenzie. In January of 1999, the Alberta Court of Appeal heard the case. That March, it upheld Medhurst's verdict.

"In hindsight," Boyd Craig reflects, "we were so fortunate not to get [Alberta] the first time. Because then we would have been partnered with David Mackenzie!"

13

A-Channel, Eh?

There are nights when the yellow moon draws close to the earth under a velvet sky and seems to smile benignly on humanity. September 20, 1997, was that kind of night in Calgary—at least at the corner of Seventh Avenue and Fifth Street. The LRT commuter train that usually rumbles along Seventh for once was silent. The air was laced instead with explosions of icy-hot notes from the fingers of Colin James as he made love to his electric guitar. When that stopped, there were literal explosions in the night sky: for half an hour, dazzling fireworks were reflected in the mirrored glass of Calgary's downtown skyscrapers.

Inside an 80-metre white tent occupying the middle of the intersection, servers offered champagne to the invited guests lined up at the hot buffet. Here and there, camera crews moved about capturing the moment: the swirl and sequins of Calgary's glitterati, the boogie swing of James's music. For those Calgarians who weren't there in person, the party was going out live—on the city's first new television station in twenty-three years. Impossible to ignore above every head was the two-storey illuminated "A" rising up the corner façade of the heritage building that was Craig Broadcast's new home in Alberta. A-Channel had arrived.

It had been eight months of incredible intensity for the Craig team to get A-Channel on the air. At first, there had been only Drew and Jodi (the couple had moved to Calgary in June) and a couple of key executives from MTN—Al Thorgeirson, its general manager, and Cam Cowie, its sales manager. Joanne Levy had accepted a contract to administer the Drama Fund. There had been the usual head-spinning list of priorities, all of them urgent. There was a plant to acquire—in fact, there were *two* plants to acquire. There were people to hire as well. So many applications flooded in for 300 positions that the A-Channel team resorted to tossing them into boxes by category: engineering;

on-air; front-office; news. There were definitive schedules to draw up (unique in each city) and programs to buy.

And, inevitably, there were delays. The Craig plan relied on A-Channel making its presence felt right away. Part of that plan was to locate studios in the heart of each city's downtown. Buildings were found in both places, but they needed complete renovation.

Drew wanted A-Channel to be Canada's first all-digital TV operation from the moment of sign-on. "An issue," he remembers, "was getting technology that was forward-compatible enough for high-definition TV. There was a lot of risk involved in terms of making a commitment to the right format." In early spring, Craig signed the first North American order for a completely digital, turn-key suite of studio electronics from Japan's industry-leading Sony. (To Drew's disappointment, though, Craig would not be able to claim the first all-digital operation *on-air:* Baton's new CIVT-TV in Vancouver scooped that honour by four days.) As it was, the folks from Sony were hard-pressed to meet Craig's timeline. On the afternoon of the launch, Drew recalls, "Sony was still in there wiring things and hooking things up."

A-Channel had promised to bring something new to Alberta TV screens. The search for shows to fulfill that commitment produced one last brush with CanWest Global. The incident gave some hint of how determined Asper remained to get a tap into Alberta's revenue stream. CanWest Global offered Craig a schedule of strong shows to which it owned Canadian rights. But there were conditions. Global wanted to hold back some avails in the shows it proposed to sell Craig so that it could sell that time itself. *And* it wanted to represent Craig nationally, reaping an additional 5 to 10 per cent commission from every national ad placed on any of the family's stations. "We just said 'No,'" Boyd Craig recalls drily. Instead, Craig went into partnership with an existing "rep-house," pumping in equity to expand its operations and renaming the business Craig Airtime Sales; it operates now out of Toronto.

There had even been moments in the launch of the new Alberta stations that brought back tense memories of Portage la Prairie. The transmitter for the Calgary station was built in Ontario and was to be assembled on-site. "It was rolling down the highway on a flatbed five days before we signed on," Drew recalls. Once it was put together, the unit gave them one last heart spasm when (further shades of Manitoba) a critical tube blew out during the transmitter's "burn-in" period. It as not an unusual event when new transmitters were first run up to power. But it meant that the New York–based manufacturer had to charter a specialized cargo plane to fly a replacement to Alberta—the fragile tube in its packing case was too big to fit in the door of a regular jet.

For all the tension, pressure and uncertainty, Drew Craig reflects, "I didn't sense it as a hardship. It wasn't nearly as hectic as putting MTN on the air." In fact, Drew, Jodi, Thorgeirson, Levy, Lisa Meeches—the whole Craig team—had just come off an exhilarating eight-month roller-coaster ride. Blushing a little, Drew admits: "It was so much fun. Everybody who signed on got the buzz. It made us feel, 'We've got to do this again!'"

There had really been only one small blot on the merriment of either opening. It had happened in Edmonton. Recalled Stuart Craig: "Goddamn him if Samy [Salloum] didn't crash the party!" Salloum's case against Craig had already been dismissed as worthless by the Alberta Court of Queen's Bench, but Salloum had appealed the matter. Stuart's blue eyes blazed as he remembered: "I had the pleasure of physically grabbing him by the arm and throwing him out of there." (Reminded of this incident, Drew Craig amends the account only slightly to say that Stuart had willing backup from his boys: "I think all three of us shared the honours on that one!")

Twenty-three months later, the happy scene of celebration was repeated at the Forks in Winnipeg. Another magical night brought hundreds of Manitoba movers and shakers, including newly elected and not-yet sworn-in NDP Premier Gary Doer, to mingle with Catherine Moffat, Bob Cornell and other Craig friends and family as they toasted the rebranding of MTN as "A-Channel Manitoba"—and the station's long-sought arrival in the heart of the provincial capital. Remembering the long battle to expand outside of Brandon, Stuart could justly claim vindication: "I thought eventually we'd get permission. I thought eventually we'd have studios in Winnipeg. It's all happening."

That, and much more. The company that had been losing money with 18 employees when Johnny B. Craig bought CKX in 1948 turned fifty under family management with 600 employees and a bottom line that was gratifyingly healthy.

The business that began it all, radio, had changed greatly in the interim. Live "event" broadcasts were long gone, giving way first to chatterbox deejays spinning discs and punching up the "time-and-temp," and later to banks of computers that barely needed the touch of a human hand from one hour to the next. In 1999, the first radio station ever to send a signal across the wheatfields of southwestern Manitoba, CKX-AM, received permission to go off the air; its programming moved to the FM band. That gave Craig two FM services in its hometown. Together with separate pairs of stations in Regina and Winnipeg (where CFQX-FM and CKMM-FM were among the city's top listening choices), that side of the business was turning over a million dollars a year in profit.

MDS wireless cable was proving more of a challenge. There had been heavy capital costs involved in erecting additional microwave towers. And the first generation of set-top receivers that Craig's SkyCable Inc. received from their Manitoba manufacturer had proven disappointing. (Another supplier now provides upgraded units.) The CRTC rebuffed an application to extend the service into southern Ontario; late in 1997 it gave that licence instead to Look TV, a subsidiary of Quebec giant Teleglobe Inc.

In Manitoba, however, an adjustment in marketing strategy was starting to take hold. SkyCable dropped installation fees, priced wireless cable below the coaxial kind and began pushing its technical advantages—including extremely fast, broadband, two-way Internet access. "It wasn't too much fun in the beginning," Miles Craig acknowledges of wireless cable. "But it's going to be good for us."

It may also be a ticket to wider horizons still for the broadcasters from Brandon. In late 1998, Stuart renewed his interest in the potential of the U.S. Southwest during a trip to Palm Springs, California, to accept an award as "Communications Entrepreneur of the Year" from accounting firm Ernst and Young. As if to live up to the award on the spot, Stu took the opportunity to scope out and acquire an existing analogue MDS wireless-cable network in the wealthy California community. The plan was to upgrade it to provide digital service.

Weeks later, Stuart travelled again, this time with Boyd, to New Zealand. Communications infrastructure in that country lags behind Canada's. The Craigs were able to acquire rights to key microwave "spectrum" to which regulators had attached no specific purpose: it could be used to deliver wireless cable, as a high-speed Internet service provider, or even for telephony transmission. In late 1999, Boyd skipped the A-Channel Manitoba launch party in order to return to New Zealand and explore ways to develop the newly acquired spectrum.

Meanwhile, SkyCable will help anchor the family's long-sought move into the heart of Winnipeg. As the new century began, renovation crews were at work on an elegant eight-storey granite edifice steps away from Portage and Main in Winnipeg's heritage Exchange District. The former Great West Life building dates from the early 1900s, the same era in which Alexander Craig and his young brood sailed from Scotland. Old Alex's great-grandchildren will fill one of its floors with SkyCable Inc. Their two Winnipeg radio stations will have studios on the high-ceilinged third floor. Another tenant is likely to be the local office of Craig Airtime Sales.

But ask the Craigs, collectively or individually, who they *are,* and they won't tell you "landlords," or "investors," or "deal-makers." They'll tell you: "We're broadcasters." Radio and television remain the heart of their business.

As rich as the Alberta foothills had looked from a distance, the family had taken an enormous risk in launching not one but *two* new stations at the same time. In a single stroke, they had doubled the size of Craig Broadcast Systems.

As with any new station, A-Channel was expected to need time to find its audience. But Craig Broadcast invested heavily to promote its mix of new prime-time movies, second-run syndicated hits like *Frasier* and *Friends* running five evenings a week, and *Canadian Movie Night.* High-intensity, live local programming, including a weekday morning storefront variety and news show called *The Big Breakfast,* was calculated to involve viewers as directly as possible.

Around Calgary and Edmonton, A-Channel's highly visible yellow-and-black "Hummer" Humvee news cruisers stamped the station's identity on the streets in a highly visible way in even the worst Alberta weather. The Edmonton station scored a coup when Drew acquired local broadcast rights to the NHL Oilers' home games. A-Channel's Calgary newsroom scored another when its News@Six package won a CANPRO award in 1999 as Canada's best nightly local newscast.

By spring 1999, CKAL-TV led Calgary's ratings in prime-time. The Craigs' financial risk began to pay off as CKAL and its sister station, CKEM-TV Edmonton, together with their rebroads in Lethbridge and Red Deer, went cash-positive during their second year, right on plan.

Johnny B. Craig had stood on the doorstep of an age of prodigious innovation. Along with sputniks, transistors and microwaves, the twenty years that followed his gamble on broadcasting transformed the industry from a monoculture of AM radio to a jostling bazaar of competing AM and FM (mainly stereo) radio stations and (increasingly in colour) television, both off air and on cable. For many of those years, it had been all Craig and his son could do just to keep Western Manitoba Broadcasters in the game, let alone in family hands.

As the century drew to a close, the founder's grandsons looked toward a future that promised to be no less tumultuous. Less than a decade old, the Internet was already drawing millions of viewers ("surfers," they were called on the World Wide Web) away from their televisions. Advertising dollars were beginning to follow them in numbers significant enough for other media to worry about. If on-line audio and video streaming technologies continued to advance at the pace established in the 1990s, it was possible that, not too far into the new century, broadcast television itself might become as relevant as semaphores were in the age of "wireless telegraphy." Drew, Boyd and Miles Craig would clearly need all the accumulated family wisdom they could muster to navigate the years ahead.

By 1999 Drew was running the family's television interests, with Boyd weighing in on financials. "Drew is the creative guy," his father said, assessing his sons' strength and weaknesses. "He loves television, knows all the programs, all the program distributors, every show that's being made." It is Drew—and his wife, Jodi, the former host of *F.I.T.*—who will determine the look and feel of the company's on-screen identity as A-Channel.

Boyd? "He's a wheeler-dealer," observed Stu. "Every time I look around he's bought something else. He's always made a good deal." In addition to directly overseeing the Craig radio chain, Boyd plays a corporate role in raising capital and in growing SkyCable, the wireless company.

After a lengthy emotional illness that was successfully contained, Miles is reevaluating his position in the company.

One thing unlikely to change is a business style that evolved around the kitchen table in Brandon. Nowadays it relies on cel-phones. "We don't have too many formal sit-downs," notes Boyd. "We do talk on the phone a lot."

But the Craigs are not numbers people. "I don't think we've ever run the numbers on anything to convince ourselves it's a good thing. We do it for the banks," says Boyd. "You can do all the numbers you want, but those numbers will never work out as you planned."

Drew agrees. "There's lots of bean-counters [in broadcasting]," he reflects. "A lot of people in the upper echelons who have no interest in what's going on the air. And it's not a bean-counting business. It's a content business." All three brothers insist sibling rivalry gets parked at the boardroom door. "We've always gotten along really well together, worked well together," says Miles.

"It never gets ugly," Boyd observes. "It's strictly business."

Adds Drew: "We're not always on the same page; in fact, we rarely are. We've had some very colourful discussions. But we can have a heated debate, then walk out the door and go home to dinner and not think about it."

It helps that all three Craigs share an attitude to business that, while never losing sight of the seriousness of the stakes, is nonetheless playful. "We all enjoy business," notes Miles. "It's not 'work' to us. It's fun."

But there are differences among the three—and weaknesses. Boyd admits to an unruly impatience. "I think things are easier than they actually are," he says. His brothers sometimes plead with him to suspend his penchant for snap decisions.

Drew, by family consensus, "just loves to spend money." Says Boyd of the way his older brother put A-Channel on the air in Alberta: "I wouldn't have built a TV station like that. They're very, very expensive, very well-appointed studios: we blew the budget." Still, Boyd offers in his brother's defence that "from the operational viewpoint, we're right *on* budget."

As the waning months of radio's century slipped away, it was clear that Stuart's daily advice and sage experience would not be available much longer. The cancer that he had beaten back once before returned in early 1999, this time in his pancreas. By summer, his once-heavy figure was rail thin.

In October 1999, in a rare act of personal self-indulgence, Stuart made a trip he had dreamed of since he was a young man. With no business in mind, only a tourist's pleasure, he travelled to Japan for ten days, taking along his sister Catherine and her husband. Less than three weeks after their return, on Saturday, October 30, Stuart Craig died in Brandon.

He had been too modest a man to fit the title "tycoon." He was someone who took pride and satisfaction in repanelling the bathroom at the cottage, in mulching the large garden behind the grey split-level on Cedar Bay Crescent, in baking a mouth-watering blueberry pie.

Friends like Stuart's old hockey and land-development partner Bob Cornell remembered "a very honest person, a very honourable business guy. Money wasn't all that important to him."

Former adversaries agreed. "One of the good ones has gone," said Ken Clark, who worked with Craig when both managed CBC affiliates and then competed against him as manager of Moffat's CKY-TV in Winnipeg. "I found him to be a very straight shooter." At the time of his death, Stuart had been scheduled to be inducted into the Canadian Association of Broadcasters' national Hall of Fame, at that body's autumn convention.

Around Brandon, small signs reveal the extent of Craig's discreet generosity in response to virtually every community fund-raising call for the last quarter-century. At the Brandon General Hospital, Craig Broadcast Systems Inc. leads the list of patrons and donors. The Craig family name also attaches to a scholarship endowed in Shirley's memory at Brandon University. The school's director of development, Beth Proven, calls the Craigs "very significant and very good friends of the university."

Looking back on his own record shortly before his death, Stuart saw more "opportunities I've missed than mistakes I've made." Among the latter was his failure to recognize the potential of cable in time to get into the game. The missed opportunities included a shot at CHCH-TV Hamilton, which came up at the wrong time in the late 1980s (Craig's cash flow was tied up at the time in trying to lift the Portage la Prairie station into the black), and the difficult decision in the early 1990s to forgo a lead role in the Women's Television Network (WTN) in order to concentrate instead on Alberta.

Only one criticism seemed to carry much sting. Stuart always believed the CRTC did not award Craig Broadcast a Vancouver licence in 1997 in part because commissioners doubted whether the family company was up to its commitments. "I think they felt we had too much on our plate," he flared. "They forgot who we were. We've got experience in this thing. Everything we ever said we'd do, we've done."

One challenge Stuart's sons should not face again is a crisis over corporate control. The legalities of an anticipated Craig succession were carefully planned by Stuart and Shirley together, before the latter's death. Stuart's will left each son an equal, one-third share of the family holding company. If the tax-planners have done their work, the inheritances should be free of any further duties or taxes.

The emotional blow will be harder to weather. "Somebody who was your dad, your friend and your partner in business, somebody you looked up to," Drew reflects. "It's tough to think what it's going to be like."

"It's lonely sometimes," Boyd concedes. "I think, 'Damn, who am I going to call?'" In addition to a wise counsellor, the third generation has lost a respected arbiter. "We haven't had any major blow-ups," Boyd observes. "But my dad was always around to police it. I don't know what will happen now that he's not around."

Still, there seemed every reason to accept Miles's assessment: "He taught us well," he says of the father who hashed out business strategy with Shirley and the kids over Shreddies. The proof of that will lie in the years ahead.

As much as Craig Broadcast Systems has grown, it is still among the smallest players in the North American broadcasting universe.

To put the company in perspective, Craig's revenues at the end of the century were about one-quarter of 1 per cent of those being generated by the industry leader: the behemoth created by the $55-billion September 1999 merger of Viacom Inc. (owner of the American UPN television network) and CBS Corporation (till that time, the world's largest purely media company). Even among station groups in English Canada, the Craigs' four television outlets in two provinces placed them far behind the smallest of their rivals. The soon-to-be-dismembered WIC, as well as CanWest Global, CTV and CHUM/CITY, all owned more stations—WIC and CTV, more than twice as many—and pulled in annual revenues at least four times as large as Craig's.

"In order to survive," says Drew Craig, "we will need to expand our critical mass or exit the industry. Most of the pioneer smaller market broadcasters in Canada have had to take that route."

The alternative is to become major-market broadcasters themselves. And in mid-1999, the CRTC presented an opportunity for the Craigs to do just that. It called again for proposals to provide a new television service in the Vancouver and Vancouver Island region.

Generations of Chinese immigrants have called British Columbia "Golden Mountain." It still seemed not a bad description. While many residents complained that their economy had hit a wall in the nineties under a scandal-plagued New Democratic government, broadcasters in the lower B.C. mainland had watched revenues climb by 10.5 per cent in 1997 and then 13.5 per cent in 1998. Despite Baton's entry into the market with CIVT-TV, Vancouver-area broadcasters were earning pre-tax margins of 24 per cent, two-thirds higher than the industry's Canada-wide average. In addition to the $200 million that incumbent Canadian outlets in the Vancouver "EM" (extended market) were drawing in, an estimated $15 million a year more flowed across the border to KVOS-TV in Bellingham, Washington.

But if the Vancouver market was richer than ever, the competitive field was even more confused.

WIC was technically still the biggest player, with its enormously dominant BCTV franchise built on CHAN-TV in Vancouver, as well as the unusual privilege of a second station in the market: CHEK-TV, in Victoria. But as the fifth year after Frank Griffiths Sr.'s death passed, his empire remained in a sort of limbo that caused those working for it growing anguish. "It is becoming increasingly difficult to run WIC as an ordinary business," Grant Buchanan wrote to the CRTC in a plaintive letter. "With shareholders issues overhanging day-to-day operations, uncertainty places additional stress on the staff. The delays also make it difficult to hire and retain executive talent. WIC's employees are now reporting to their third C.E.O. and second Chairman since this process started a year ago. Two successive chief financial officers have left."

Founder Frank Griffiths's widow, Emily, confronted by her son's inability to fill his father's shoes, sold her control stake in the company in March 1998. In the normal course of events, that should have handed WIC's stick to someone new, or at the very least opened the door to a break-up sale.

Curiously, neither happened.

The reason was a strange, three-way standoff that involved the children of the late Frank Griffiths Sr.'s Edmonton partner, Dr. Charles Allard; a second-generation Calgary family of cable operators; and Izzy Asper.

The latter's CanWest Global Corp. had, over the years, collected a considerable holding in WIC B shares. By 1999 it held the largest single chunk of that stock, some 30 per cent. But it was impotent equity. B shares held no vote—unless a change in control of the company triggered the "coat-tail" in WIC's bylaws, converting B shares to voting A's. CanWest had even gone to court once to argue that Emily

Griffiths had triggered the coat-tail by selling the Allards a larger, but still minority, voting stake in the company in the mid-nineties. The court had not bitten. Neither had Emily herself, when Asper put various offers before her to buy out her shares.

When Griffiths's widow *did* sell her stake in WIC, the deal could have been purpose-designed to thwart Asper's ambitions. In a Solomonic division of the spoils, Griffiths sold her shares in two packets to Cathton Holdings Ltd. of Edmonton and Shaw Communications Inc. of Calgary. If approved by the CRTC, the division would put 49.96 per cent of WIC's voting shares in Shaw's hands, 49.9 per cent in Cathton's. Artfully, Shaw president Jim Shaw (JR's son) argued this meant that WIC had "been sold from a control position to a non-control position, because no one shareholder can control it." Hence, Shaw concluded, the coat-tail was *not* triggered. Equally, CanWest's B shares remained exactly that: *non-voting* B shares.

But the truth of the situation was more like a bus teetering on the edge of a precipice. Cathton, the Allard family vehicle, does not actually *run* anything. Shaw does, but it had vocally forsworn any control over WIC. (Its experience, moreover, is in operating cable and specialty channels, not in broadcasting.) Meanwhile, there was the sticky matter of CanWest's B stock and the strong possibility Asper would try again to have the court declare the coat-tail triggered. This time, he might well have a case.

In August 1998, a brief press release from WIC disclosed that a resolution was at hand. The company's "two largest [total equity] shareholders, Shaw Communications Inc. and CanWest Global Corp.," it announced, "have come to a preliminary agreement concerning WIC." (But it would take until October 1999, fourteen months later, for the parties to resolve their differences.)

The deal would transfer WIC's television assets, including such crown jewels as CHAN Vancouver, ON-TV Hamilton and CFCF Montreal, to CanWest. With WIC's Alberta stations, Izzy would finally and unequivocally have his "national" network, although he would also be in the ticklish position of owning three TV licences in essentially the same extended Vancouver market (Global's existing CKVU, plus WIC's CHAN and CHEK), as well as dual licences in Ontario and Montreal. Shaw would have less difficulty absorbing the radio, satellite service and specialty TV interests that made up the rest of WIC, and was likely to see some cash out of the deal.

Were it approved and consummated, WIC's dismemberment would be likely to trigger a series of other realignments. Speculation at the time of writing was that the commission might well sign off on the overall transaction but would almost certainly direct CanWest to give up at least one and possibly two of its Vancouver-area stations, as well as the extra Hamilton and Montreal licences. CanWest and Shaw were required to file their applications to the CRTC by December 1999. But with hearings scheduled for April 2000, the commission's consideration of the whole complex package could easily be delayed into the last half of the year 2000.

The corporation-formerly-known-as-Baton was also at the table. Late in 1998, Baton had renamed itself "CTV Inc." Now its president and CEO, Ivan Fecan was in the process of fusing the old Baton chain with five of the original seven sisters of the former co-op network, which it now owned. Vancouver was an anomaly on CTV's map. Its local network affiliate there was WIC's booming CHAN, while its own start-up, CIVT, was struggling to find an audience. Logic suggested that when CHAN's CTV affiliation agreement next came up for renewal, CTV might be inclined to reclaim it for its own station.

But who knew for sure? It was all speculation. And until the CanWest/Shaw deal was actually put in front of the CRTC, all of it was so much dancing on moonbeams. Whatever fate awaited the existing licences in Vancouver and Victoria, none was likely to come on the market soon.

Besides, as the Craigs deeply appreciated, opening their own new station would not only be a whole lot more fun, in the long run it would also provide a much better return. "Our preference," says Drew, "is to start with a clean piece of paper. To create your own service is the best way to create value for a company."

Stuart had shared his son's view: "We started the stations in Alberta for $20 million," he recalled. "If we were to sell them to Izzy, he'd have to pay $200 million [based on established industry price/earnings multiples]. Which would you rather do?"

But there was yet a third reason to prefer a fresh start to entering an auction for someone else's cast-off asset. With each new application, each opportunity to create a new television presence, the Craigs's vision had become better defined and more ambitious. The application Craig Broadcast Systems Inc. filed on September 23, 1999, on the eve of the party at the Forks launching A-Channel Manitoba, was in many ways the family's most refined and far-reaching statement of its vision yet.

In an echo of that overworked new-age maxim to "Think globally; act locally," Craig Broadcast was claiming a specific and vital role in the nation's television culture, while still rooting its identity firmly in a bone-deep sense of local community.

It was to be called "A-Channel on the Island." It would be based in Victoria, British Columbia's capital and oldest city, but its local programming was designed to reflect all the diverse communities of 450-kilometre-long Vancouver Island. To be viable, however, Craig Broadcast argued that the new station's coverage—and its advertising sales effort—must include the entire Vancouver extended market.

Craig planned to capitalize a new subsidiary with $20 million to launch the proposed service—as much as it had spent on the two new Calgary stations combined. TD Capital was on board again, for 33.3 per cent. Craig Broadcast would put up the rest itself—and hold the balance of the equity.

By the filing deadline, five competing applicants were also before the CRTC. For once, CanWest Global was not among them. Three proposals, in fact, came from the same source. CHUM's Moses Znaimer, a frequent Craig ally, submitted separate applications for a Vancouver station and a Victoria station with a rebroadcaster that would beam Victoria's signal into Vancouver. Other bids came from Rogers (which once again proposed a multicultural format, this time a start-up) and, unusually, from a Winnipeg-based Christian group, Trinity Television.

The application most directly competitive with Craig's was the three-pack that Znaimer had entered. A-Channel collaborated often with CITY-TV in acquiring packages of U.S. movies. CHUM was frequently Joanne Levy's first call when she sought to round up national exposure for A-Channel's Drama Fund productions. But if it troubled Drew Craig from Brandon to go toe to toe with the philosopher-executive from Queen Street, it didn't show. "Guys, no hard feelings, but the call's there" was Drew's attitude. "We're going to be there. The best scenario for you is that you win. The second-best scenario for you is that *we* win. Good luck."

Luck would play a role. It always does. But the winning application would need more than that.

One particular passage of the A-Channel proposal provided a glimpse of the values that stood behind the Craig application. In prose almost too poetic for a legal document, it introduced the commission to Vancouver Island's story from the beginning. Not the colonial beginning, but the real one: the days when the Salish, Nuu-chah-nulth and Kwakwaka'wakw First Nations ruled the misty cedars of the western rainforest.

"Living on an island has an effect on people," the application observed. "This both bonds island people together and encourages a more independent overall outlook on things. The fact that people choose to live on an island reflects certain values and a different set of priorities in life. Taken together, they become the basis of a distinct community with a unique character and identity."

The application went on to offer some observations about that identity:

- "Individuals stand out and make a difference. Islanders are very fond of 'eccentrics' and larger-than-life characters who speak their mind. If what they say makes sense, they usually elect them to something."
- "Islanders love the sea and everything about it . . . have a strong sense of the arts and . . . a great affinity for the outdoors and the preservation of nature."
- "Victorians tend to speak 'for the Island' but in doing so, often overlook the interests of the up-island communities."
- "Islanders are very independent people, mavericks who often go their own way. This makes them 'creative' if you agree with their ends, and 'trouble-makers' if you don't."
- "Finally, there is a general feeling . . . that bigger is not always better."

A-Channel, Craig argued, would fit right in.

"What does the 'A' in A-Channel mean?" its application read. "As the first letter of the alphabet, 'A' has always connoted something of superior quality. But to Craig, it means much more. The name 'A-Channel' connotes the idea of being 'alternative,' 'adventurous,' 'accurate,' and 'accessible.'" Corny, but you couldn't argue with the goals.

A-Channel on the Island framed its commitments to the island's maverick, free-thinking community—and to their proxy jury of CRTC panelists—on three levels.

The identity of the new station would rest on programming for and by the people of Vancouver Island. There would be twice the number of hours of local news a week that CHEK aired. A news bureau in Nanaimo would be the base for a special effort to give "up-island" balance. There would be a local version of the highly successful *Big Breakfast* morning show format, as well as prime-time programs on business and B.C. politics. *Two Five-0* (the Vancouver Island area code) would be a daily showcase for Island entertainers. A west-coast edition of Lisa Meeches's *The Sharing Circle* (the longest-running aboriginal magazine show in Canada was entering its eighth season in Manitoba) would bring a fresh, positive perspective to the simmering conflict between British Columbia natives and non-natives.

The second part of the plan rested on A-Channel's growing capacity to open new broadcast windows for creative expression across the whole Canadian West. The application proposed to join A-Channel on the Island with its Alberta and Manitoba sister-stations for a live, hour-long daily interview show targetting newsmakers relevant to the West. The Victoria studios would also contribute items to the larger system's *Great Big Saturday Morning* show—a chatty mix of cartoons and kid-oriented live-action breaks. More significantly, the Victoria studio would become home to its own, full-scale regional show. *Entertainment West,* a weekly magazine and variety program "showcasing Canadian entertainment," would be broadcast from Victoria to all A-Channel stations as a lead-in to their popular signature Sunday evening show, *Canadian Movie Night.* The idea, Craig said, was to pick up on a challenge the CRTC had set in its revision of the country's television policy earlier in the year, by "foster[ing] a Western Canada star system."

But it was part three of the proposal that showed how clearly—and imaginatively—the Craigs have thought through their potential role in the national broadcasting system. The application noted two facts. One was the commission's own declaration in its TV policy revisions in June 1999 that the so-called "priority" categories of Canadian programs—drama, music and variety, and long-form documentaries—continued to be underfunded. The second was that, since its inception barely two years earlier, Craig's A-Channel Drama Fund in Alberta had given broadcast-licence "green lights" to nine completed movies and supported another two dozen long-form projects with script and development funding. "Over the term of our Alberta licence," the Craig proposal stated, "we fully expect to cause to be created over forty made-in-Alberta 2-hour films. This is an incredible success story."

A-Channel on the Island aimed to double that number of productions in the categories the CRTC had defined as national priorities.

Specifically, a new fund would spend $12.7 million over the term of the licence to buy national broadcast rights for "as many as forty Canadian television movies, mini-series and other drama programs, and as many as forty new long-form documentaries." British Columbia producers would go to the head of the line. Together with its own productions like *Entertainment West*, Craig proposed to spend nearly $26 million on "priority" programs over its licence term.

Those were the numbers. There was also a little Craig attitude.

The application noted that the CRTC had decided in June to raise the bar for "large broadcast groups" by increasing the minimum amount of Canadian television content they were required to air in prime-time (between 7:00 and 11:00 p.m.) to at least eight hours a week. By the CRTC's definition, only CTV, Global and WIC, among English-language broadcasters, had the audience reach to qualify as "large groups" and incur the new obligations. Craig, even with a presence in B.C., would be less than half the size of the smallest of them. But it was ready to play by the big boys' rules. By the end of its licence term, little Craig Broadcast from Brandon undertook to program prime-time Canadian shows at the same "large group" rate as CTV and CanWest Global.

And there was one more thing.

"Unlike the other multi-station groups," the Craig application mentioned, "we expect that a majority of our Canadian programs will emanate from Western Canada. Just as important, the decisions to acquire or produce those programs will be taken entirely in Western Canada."

The CRTC scheduled hearings on the British Columbia licence for February 2000. The men and women of its broadcast panel would weigh Craig Broadcast's bid against those of Rogers, CHUM and Trinity and apply the test of the Broadcasting Act. It would be up to them to decide which company would "maintain and enhance national identity and cultural sovereignty" well enough to merit a seven-year licence for a scarce television channel.

14

Values to Build On

"In anybody's career as a broadcaster," observes Drew Craig, "you want to *launch*. It's a moment you never forget. When you sit back and look at it and say, 'There it is!'" He pauses. "Stu launched four stations. I've done three."

Part of the thrill, Craig admits, is the knowledge that "They never go off. They're forever."

On December 12, 2001, it will be one hundred years since Guglielmo Marconi sat in a drafty stone tower on a bluff overlooking St. John's harbour and strained to hear, through the crackle of static, three simple clicks. The letter 'S' in the Morse alphabet.

On the anniversary of that day, it won't be a single letter crossing space on electromagnetic waves. There will be a near-infinity of them. Now, data streams by the millions flicker invisibly through every cubic centimetre of space. Radios were just the start of it, in AM and FM shortwave and sideband and UHF versions. Then came television, pagers and cel-phones. Remote-controlled toy airplanes. Images and e-mail. And enough e-cash washing from Geneva to the Nikkei on any given day to purchase the developing economy of your choice.

Broadcasting is still an affair of wiring and show business, money and nerves. If anything, the risks keep getting higher. The accelerating cycle of technological change renders each generation of capital plant obsolete even sooner than the last one. Markets divide and subdivide and microdivide, as entirely new diversions like virtual-reality gaming and Internet chat-rooms lure audiences from the 500-channel megaplex waiting at their TV's clicker-tip.

The Internet, in fact, threatens to be a technological Trojan Horse of unimaginable potency. Already only a mouse-click away are dozens of Web-based "radio" stations (mostly American) and amateur as well as professional "live-cam" and video streams. For the moment, the sound crackles, and the pictures are the size of Post-it notes. But full-screen

Web-TV with hi-fi sound beyond the reach of the most ambitious regulator is only a matter of time and bandwidth.

Amid all the turbulence, what are the odds of a small-town family company staying afloat into a second century, let alone becoming a force big enough to challenge Canada's broadcasting citadels?

Pretty good, actually.

"How do you differentiate yourself from everybody else on the dial?" Drew poses the question. "It's content. The local shows you produce are what make the connection to the viewer and establish what you are. You create something unique in the market."

In the century since Marconi, communication has become a commodity. The evidence lies in the plummeting price of a long-distance call, the insignificant cost of an e-mail compared to a stamp and an envelope. Hardware was the frontier of the last century. The future belongs to what the hardware carries: the content. The stories.

From the biggest cities to the smallest hamlets, Canadians will define themselves by those stories. To paraphrase Keith Spicer, our *stories* are Canada. For the Craigs, that is more than a maxim: It is an operating principle.

They are betting the farm on those stories.

Acknowledgements

I was having a drink with Scott McIntyre, president of Douglas & McIntyre, when he popped the question: Would I be interested in writing the history of a family company? That depended, I told him, on whether or not the family had an interesting story to tell.

As I became better acquainted with the Craig family of Brandon, Manitoba (a place I had never been), I did indeed find their story interesting, even compelling. In an age of media dominated by three North American cities (only one of them in Canada) and preoccupied by the amplified lives of celebrity super-egos, too many stories about protagonists on the smaller stages get missed. That is a great loss, because these are often stories well worth the telling. The best of them introduce us to courageous and creative people in whom we can recognize ourselves. I found this to be that kind of story.

There was something else Scott McIntyre wanted me to know before I assented to the project. This was to be a "commissioned" history, meaning the subjects would ultimately foot the bill. This, both he and a number of other friends advised me, could possibly cast a negative shadow across my journalistic reputation. After thinking it over, I agreed to take the assignment.

I sell stories for a living, have done for most of my life. It's an honourable trade with a long lineage. In the past quarter of a century, I have at different times sold poetry, radio and television scripts, fiction, commercial copy and more magazine articles than I can remember. All were stories of one sort or another, and I always learned a thing or two from the experience. There are a hundred different ways to be paid for a story. There are a thousand ways to tell one. But there is only one way to tell a story right, whatever form it takes: truthfully. I have tried to do that here.

The events in this book have been established from both first-hand and documentary sources. I am indebted to several particularly useful published and unpublished histories of radio in Canada, including Marv Vipond's excellent *Listening In* (1992), and the self-published and out-of-print memoir of western broadcasting pioneer T. J. Allard, *Straight Up*. Other documentation was found at the Daly House (Brandon) Museum when I travelled to Manitoba to research the Craig family on their home ground. CRTC hearings are reconstructed from transcripts; other portions of the narrative draw on the private correspondence and files of the late Stuart Craig. In addition, Stuart, before his death, as well as Drew, Boyd and Miles Craig, provided me with extensive interviews covering many hours.

I want to thank the Craigs for their candour and their trust. However pointed my questioning over many hours of interviews, there was never a moment when they refused to explore any aspect of their family or corporate history that I felt needed to be examined. Their review of the manuscript corrected many small errors.

I wish also to thank Robert Lewis, the editor of *Maclean's,* who kindly released me on a leave of absence during a busy news period in order to undertake this book.

My wife (and, on other projects, my writing partner as well), Beverley Wood, knows that she has my undying gratitude for putting up with the psychosis that begins to consume a writer after too many long days at the keyboard, especially as deadline approaches.

Finally, my admiration and gratitude go to Barbara Pulling, the consummately professional editor who brought a tautness to the final manuscript it would not otherwise have possessed.

The accomplishments recorded in these pages belong to others. The shortcomings in the telling are all mine.

Chris Wood
November 1999

Index